THE COMING OF THE BODY

The Coming of the Body

Hervé Juvin
Translated by John Howe

VERSO
London • New York

Ouvrage publié avec le concours du Ministère français
chargé de la culture—Centre national du livre
This work was published with the help of the French
Ministry of Culture—Centre national du livre

This edition first published by Verso 2010

First published as *L'avènement du corps*

1 3 5 7 9 10 8 6 4 2

Verso
UK: 6 Meard Street, London W1F 0EG
US: 20 Jay Street, Suite 1010, Brooklyn, NY 11201
www.versobooks.com

Verso is the imprint of New Left Books

ISBN-13: 978-1-84467-310-0

British Library Cataloguing in Publication Data
A catalogue record for this book is available from the British Library

Library of Congress Cataloging-in-Publication Data
A catalog record for this book is available from the Library of Congress

Typeset by MJ Gavan, Truro, Cornwall
Printed in the US by Maple Vail

Contents

Foreword

> Happiness lies in knowing nothing of oneself and in dying without having noticed that one was alive.
>
> Chateaubriand, *Memoirs from Beyond the Grave*, Book V, chap. VI

I used to know a rural Brittany where the peasants were worn out, broken by hard labour, at sixty. Let's not even mention the women: after the age of thirty or thirty-five, what remained to them of what we call womanhood? And I used to know a Morbihan where the furniture, the artisan's tools, the kitchen pots and pans, all the objects in daily use, witnessed the succession of human generations, the cohorts of domestic animals. The fishing tackle, the handles and blades in the workshop or outhouse, smoke-blackened, polished by the hand of the artisan, by the fist of the deep-sea fisherman or peasant, outlived the men who used them, and were worth more.

In the old Menton cemetery the youngest daughter of an Indian Army major, laid to rest at twenty-two, lies alongside a Prince Volkonsky, eighteen, a twenty-eight-year-old duke and two young Polish girls aged fourteen and seventeen—joined much later in the same burial ground by their parents, one aged eighty-six and the other eighty-four.

Elsewhere, along the Skrang River in Borneo, in the sands of the deep Kalahari, I have tasted what remains of nature, the real thing, in which a domestic animal might survive a few hours or perhaps a day, where a Western man has little chance of surviving more than a day or two without the complicated array that keeps him comfortable, but makes him into an invalid and permanent dependant.

There comes to mind the long line of deep-seam coal miners, not one of whom until the second half of the last century doubted that silicosis was gnawing slowly at his lungs—and who accepted it, when he wasn't actually proud of his cavernous cough. It was part of the calling. They were coal miners: more than a family, a calling. And death, profoundly earned, conferred on the oldest of them, seated on the benches in their allotments in the shadow of the slagheap, a form of nobility that was theirs alone.

Introduction

The great novelty of the early twenty-first century in Europe is that we have just invented a new body, one resistant to need, suffering and the effects of time. Resistant to the world too, the world of nature, of destiny.

That body is the product of a century in which progress delivered men from the physical effort of tilling the soil, carrying burdens, struggling to live. The product of a century in which medicine learned at last really to cure, in which an abundance of goods and services liberated a majority of the fortunate inhabitants of the Western world from need, while peace and prosperity enabled the greater number to forget heaven, their faith, their race and their party. It is the product of a West doomed to progress, through the ceaseless and ever more rigorous application of its technology to nature, to the world and finally to humanity. It is, for the first time, in keeping with the wishes of women, freed at last from motherhood as an inevitability, a destiny and an obligation.

That invented body is the gift left to us by a century of iron and blood: the gift of a life doubled in length. And that body has established itself over and above our individual and collective choices. It has taken power.

The attention focused on the problematic effects of this phenomenon —anxiety about retirement pensions, worry about lifestyle, adoption of the precautionary principle, etc.—masks the happy reality of advances in the general state of health of the populations in Western countries, of the physical well-being and material satisfaction of the majority. What we are discovering is the first civilization of well-being. Obsessive harping on the new freedom in relations between men and women that underlies the 'revolution in intimacy' analyzed by Anthony Giddens distracts us from the more general transformation of relations with the body, with money and with other people that make abundance, wealth, peace and technical progress possible.[1] The respectable citizen of the twenty-first century has a multiplied lifetime in front of him; he is also faced with choices that no one, anywhere, has ever had to make before—already glimpsed during the

1. See Anthony Giddens, *The Transformation of Intimacy*, Stanford University Press, 1992.

debates of the 1960s and 1970s on contraception and abortion, and the current ones on human cloning, homosexual marriage and parenthood (through adoption) for homosexual couples. Life is managed. Life is produced, and is constructed in the world of technology and method to such effect that nature is a taskmaster no longer, having become a mere argument; to such effect too that after a world of nature and destiny, we are discovering the world of choice: the world of the market. The responsibility is as intoxicating as it is frightening. Individual and collective anxiety over our ability to answer the questions posed by a longer lifespan distract our attention from the real issue: the respectable citizen of the twenty-first century is going to have to manage what no one has ever had to manage, a fund of life for which he is responsible, whose expenditure he controls, whose end he will determine.

How good it would be to be able to leave it at that! And how satisfactory, if this happy aspect of a heritage so burdensome in other ways should turn out to be unclouded by threats or challenges! The production of bodies and of life is certainly the first, but is also the biggest of the challenges posed by the twenty-first century. The data of space and time, the historical condition of humans in this century, are and will be irremediably upset by it; for the first time, the world's space is presented to us without the frontiers imposed on it by states, peoples and history, and without the laws of nature through which it imposed itself on us. For the first time, the categories of time that fixed the duration of a birth, an education, a transmission, are disappearing along with the very notion of reproduction, education and transmission. The whole sum of human knowledge is just a few mouse-clicks away; neither forgetfulness nor forgiveness is possible with infinite memory; all the conditions of being here, of being together, are being scrambled and recomposed.

This challenge places the body in a controlling position in the political, social, economic and scientific fields; a new human condition is our lot. An anthropological transformation—fruit of the liberal project—that puts at stake the mass of human relations with other humans, with what was beyond humans and with what united them, and that they are now threatened with losing—to the benefit, it is true, of an unprecedented possession of themselves. But would self-ownership be worth the penalty of losing all that?

This novelty is a new frontier that separates us from the rest of the world and from our history so far. It may make it possible to foresee a future conflict between the civilization of the body and the civilizations of history. Those civilizations expect the passage of time and the rising generations to lead to a better future, a revelation or a saviour. They believe in a beyond that can only be preferable to this world and this life in these bodies. What we expect is for time to stop, in a long-lasting little death: in the ecstasy of our wealth, our well-being, our contentment with ourselves. And we hope secretly that those who announce the end of history are right, so aware are we that the century to come is unlikely to be better for us if it is different, so true is it that we have more to preserve than to build and more to protect than to conquer. We refrain from measuring the economic, political and social effects of a preference for the present that transforms democracy into a museum of what already exists, that prefers deliberation to decision, the rights of the individual to the will of the majority, and that is perhaps creating the conditions for the end of democracy by the very fact that it denies any idea of determining collective progress, and denies progress any right to influence individual life choices.

The absolute novelty of the early twenty-first century is that we have to manage both a body that has become our product, and an utterly unprecedented lifespan. From the viewpoint of a medieval serf or a courtier at Versailles, Buckingham Palace or Sans-Souci, we have become alien. We are human, but no longer the humans they were. As indeed to us, our great-grandfathers in the trenches of 1916, our grandfathers from the Normandy landings of 1944, the forerunners of the Korean campaign and the Vietnam war, seem as foreign as beings from another planet. Just as our rosary-clicking grandmothers, and their grandmothers worn out by childbirth, housework and worry, subject to all the obligations of belief and appearances, are as foreign to our own mothers and wives as the women in prehistoric cave-paintings. We are worlds apart, not historical worlds but worlds of bodies, of the science and religion of bodies.

Their deprived and suffering body has become our performing one, a body for pleasure and an endless initiation into all the joys of living. And this body, its rhythm and its lifespan, are going to overturn our relations with money, our patrimony and provision for the future, as they have already overturned our relations with work, as they have already transformed our identity, our difference … and as they continue to do.

After gods, after revolutions, after financial markets, the body is becoming our truth system. It alone endures, it alone remains. In it we place all our hopes, from it we expect a reality which elsewhere is leaking away. It has become the centre of all powers, the object of all expectations, even those of salvation. We are these strange, hitherto unknown humans: the people of the body.

1. The Body Is New

So what is new, at the start of the new millennium?

The body. The body we have inherited from the twentieth century has changed in time, it has changed in space, it is very close to changing its nature. The invention of the body is the formidable gift of the century just past. But it comes without an instruction manual. Our bodies are no longer as mortal, no longer as suffering, fragile and transitory as they were, and seemed fated to remain for ever. The far off has become near, the other has dissolved into the universal. The essential split of our time is not external, it is not about markets, between those who believe in them and those who do not, or between Islam and the West, it is not in technology, IT or the Internet; it has slipped into private life, touching on the hidden relation that the individual maintains, consciously or not, with his own life. Could that be why it has also passed largely unnoticed?

By changing its time and space, the body has transformed our own relations with time and space, and has also changed in its relation to itself and to what is not itself—other bodies, the mind, the soul, nature, the environment, power and authority, desire and ownership—and that change is the capital fund for many changes to come, some already here, so much so that they blind us and prevent us from seeing what we are becoming, what we have already become. It is the unexpected guest of a century seeking its history. And it is that century's master.

Of this crazy bequest we need some sort of inventory, before letting ourselves be taken in by it, or losing it altogether.

Long life

Underlying all this is long life. Long, longer than it has ever been. So long that there are many, men and women both, who do not know what to do with the dragging days of a life that has forgotten how to end. More than 81 years of average life expectancy for French women and men, 78 for the British, 75 for Americans; a demographic revolution has occurred over the last century, of which no aspect promises benefit to future generations, and whose consequences have hardly been identified, let alone experienced to the full.

Life expectancy at birth in 1900 in the so-called 'developed' countries was under 45 years (in France, 43 for men and 46 for women), and under 30 in the rest of the world—as it had been for France during the Revolution, and Western Europe in the Middle Ages (essentially of course because of high infant mortality rates, and also mortality from infectious diseases incurable at that time). Life expectancy among the cowboys who conquered the American West was under 40 years, more or less the same as that of the Indians they were culling in reluctantly conceded reservations.

In France in 2005, life expectancy at birth had reached 75.5 years for men and 84.5 for women (in Japan, 86 already!); it has been rising steadily by nearly three months a year (2.4 exactly) for two centuries. We have every reason to hope that half the little girls born in France since 2000 will live to a hundred.

The contrast between the long, very long life that we are promised and the short life of times past is dizzying, especially as there is no shortage of data in this area. King Louis XVI, on setting up in 1787 the first fire insurance company, the Royale, also gave it the right to insure human lives and caused the first mortality tables to be compiled—charts giving the estimated remaining lifespan for women and men of every age group. In those days less than 5 per cent of men lived to 70 or more. In 2010, with the Democratic US administration's healthcare insurance plan nearing adoption, questions on the nature, scale and extent over time of healthcare services for the very old are arising in all the developed countries. And they are being addressed at a time when it is reasonable to expect that a statistically significant number of pensions will have to be paid until the age of 110, since more than 5 per cent of women aged 40 in 2005 were expected to live to over 100.

A historic break

This steadily increasing life expectancy, in France and in Europe, is a recent development in the demographic long term. Because of the terrible infant mortality rate, with fewer than one child in four reaching the age of ten, average life expectancy in France or Italy was under 25 years during the French Revolution, and under 22 during the wars of religion or the Hundred Years' War; it was about the same then as it would have been

Life Expectancy at Birth in France, 1899–1999

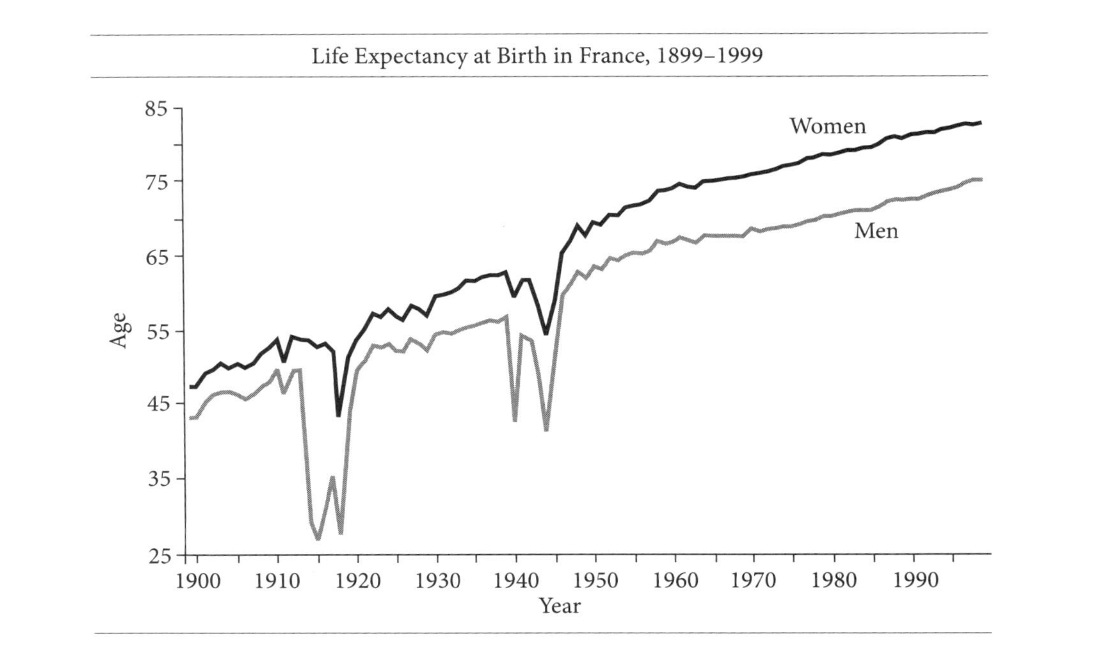

in the year 1000, or during the Roman Empire in the time of Augustus. For more than a century, between 1350 and 1450, the average lifespan throughout Europe, ravaged by successive waves of the Black Death and the movements of population and famines it caused, fell still lower to settle in the region of 19 years. The population of Europe as a whole fell from 80 million at the beginning of the fourteenth century to under 40 million around the middle of the fifteenth, abundance of food explaining the later recovery of the birth rate (the example should remind us that nothing can be taken for granted in this domain; the lengthening of lifespan is the fragile and reversible achievement of an overall sanitary and social progression, quite distinct from simple economic growth). Rather than a gradual and steady increase in the length of human life over two millennia, there was alternation between favourable periods in which peace, abundant harvests, market security and relatively easy transport brought about an improvement in the general health of the population, of which Roman Gaul supplies a lasting example, and unfavourable periods in which war, famine and the interruption of land or water transport routes sent Europe back into a more primitive way of life: soup made from weeds and bark, boiled roots and so on forming the sole diet for the majority of an enfeebled population.

We are not as remote from this as we may imagine; parts of central Europe during the advance of Soviet troops from the winter of 1943 to 1945, and parts of South-Eastern Europe—Romania, former Yugoslavia and Albania during the late 1990s—experienced food scarcity, artificial isolation and daily risk to life. And the spread of AIDS in Southern Africa reduced life expectancy there from more than 55 years to its level at the beginning of the last century of around 33. This gap in space between countries marked by such short lives and our own lands obsessed with dependence, Alzheimer's or Parkinson's, is being reduced without disappearing; if no environmental, climatic, political or epidemiological factor upsets current trends, only in the second half of the twenty-first century will life expectancy become more or less comparable on all five continents.

This break between the fragile, brief life of the last century and the long, very long life promised in this century is seen most clearly in the virtual tripling of life expectancy as a healthy adult. This was around 24 years in 1900, and 70 years on average in 2005, since the onset of predependency and dependency is now delayed until about the age of 85, on the one hand, while on the other adulthood arrives physically and psychically at an earlier age, around 14 to 16 (a study by INSERM, France's National Institute for Health and Medical Research, in March 2008 indicated that adolescents are now reaching their adult height earlier, while the average age of first sexual relations has dropped by nearly two years in half a century). At the same time, however, the economic and social maturity of young people is being delayed (especially in France, owing to delayed access to jobs and overprotective policies towards landlords, forbidding the young access to rented property without a parental guarantee). Ninety per cent of French people of both sexes aged between 60 and 80 say that they are in good health and enjoy life, at an age when most of their recent ancestors were dead. According to a European survey conducted by HSBC in 2008, men and women get the most out of life between the ages of 56 and 65. That is when the gap between what they expect from life and what they get from it is narrowest; it is at its widest between the ages of 20 and 40.

Towards unknown horizons

This break opens up the prospect of an unknown society; the gap continues to widen between the world we still remember, from which our institutions and modes of feeling and thought have come, and the universe of very long life. There is great uncertainty over future variation in the average duration of human life, but we tend to think of it in one direction only: upward. For, while the direct effects of education on nutrition and physical exercise may be enough to take average life expectancy to 100 years by 2050, in countries where average annual incomes exceed $20,000, that makes no allowance for the hopes—crazed or rational, who can tell?—raised by new technologies capable of multiplying the useful lives of some of the organs essential to life, by regenerating or replacing them, to a point where the claim 'Man is not made to die' may seem justified. 130, 180, 300 years? The possibilities raised by genetic engineering and biology, as by nanotechnologies (the implantation of subcutaneous microchips enabling biological balances to be monitored permanently in real time, diagnosis and warning signals at a distance, automatic delivery of treatments, etc.), justify such speculation on the thresholds of life in the century to come. When human lifespan has tripled in two centuries, it is no longer the same life; or the same human being.

The age breakdown of Western populations has already evolved in spectacular fashion. Europe is old in history no doubt; it is even older in its people, since it is increasingly the region of the world whose average age is the highest: 10 years more than North America, 6 to 8 years more than Asia, 20 years more than the Maghreb, 25 years more than black Africa. A whole generation will soon separate Europe from its neighbours to the South, when the median age of its population passes 50 years (in around 2050), while the median age in the Maghreb will stay below 30. Demographic growth in centuries past had but a single driving force: the women had more children, fewer of whom died in infancy. The extraordinary resistance of the French Canadians to forced assimilation had as its mainspring an exceptional fecundity; women's bellies were the rampart of Frenchness on the frontier of the world, at a time when many were mothers of 12, 15, even 18 children. For a demographic angle on the outcome of the Israeli–Palestinian conflict, a Palestinian woman has three times as many children on average as an Israeli one, and the stampeding population growth rate in some of the Gaza camps is among the highest in the world. We have brought the prodigality of life to an end; we spare every single existence. Demographic growth in Europe, in the few countries whose populations are still growing, is partly the effect of immigration, but also of the constant lengthening of lifespans; it is not that there are more births, it is that there are fewer deaths each year in the same population. And all the dreams of empire-builders and conquerors stop there, with that endless fertility now become mythical, an end to those harvests of men once fated to blossom on the fields of battle.

When the length of life doubles, it is no longer the same life, no longer the same person. This break touches more and more closely on everything connected with the duration of human life, its hazards, its brevity. For one who expects to live a century, all that has been constructed, thought out, codified to suit a short life is wrong. Everything—family, marriage, inheritance, saving, morality—needs to be shaken though a different long-life sieve. Commitment, fidelity, faith will never again have the meaning they had in societies where men were generals at 20 and eternity was waiting after another ten years: time enough to live fast and make a handsome corpse. A sort of frivolity about ourselves has gone. Life is too long now to be thrown away for nothing.

A Western privilege

The other break caused by this multiplied life expectancy is a new and more subtle separation of the world. For various reasons—alcoholism and fatalism, AIDS and poverty—life expectancy has decreased in several parts of the world since 1990. In Russia, life expectancy in 2004 was the same as in Sudan. On average, a man dies in Russia a year before reaching legal retirement age (in 2004, life expectancy for men was 59 years; the legal retirement age was 60), and average life expectancy for both sexes had dropped by more than two years over a decade (from 65 years to a little over 62, the population declining by 600,000 individuals a year mainly because of the collapse of the public health system). For other reasons, countries like Afghanistan, Haiti and Cuba are diverging sharply from the long-term tendency for lifetimes to lengthen—and from the West. Japan and Europe, firstly, and then Canada and the United States, are separating from the rest of the world through a continuous increase in life expectancy at birth, which can only be the result of collective choices upstream and individual preferences downstream arising from economic growth, choices that are seldom if ever made explicit. The preference for long life is the key to economic, political and social choices that will determine the decades to come.[1]

It would be a mistake to deduce from this that ageing is any sort of drama for Japan and Europe; for people age youthfully these days, in the West of all riches. France, so often derided for its alleged poor economic performance, has anyway achieved something of a tour de force, equalled only by Japan, by providing French people with an extra life inside a century. If French women and men had to appear in front of a 'review committee' when claiming their right to retirement, at the start of the third half-time in their lives, most would be astonished by the length of life still open to them. They have life still before them—a lifetime, at least. A man of 60, without a diagnosed illness, should plan on at least 22 years of active life before the appearance of dependence, in all its forms, becomes statistically probable and truly disabling. A woman of 60, with no identified health problem, should plan on at least 26 years of active life

1. We should note, however, that public choices differ in this area; in Europe they tend to make the extension of life expectancy an end in itself, while in the US other objectives have priority. Protestant attitudes to death may provide some clues here; see Gary Lederman's book, *The Sacred Remains: American Attitudes toward Death*, Yale University Press, 1996.

before facing the same risks. You might say that both are of an age to begin a new life together, discover new interests, learn and train, make plans, borrow money, start afresh.

The magic of beginnings is no mere memory to today's senior citizens. Youth, accompanied by the strength of maturity and undiminished joie de vivre, can now reach unknown horizons: those explored by the Egyptologist who published a book—based on his own recent research—in his ninetieth year, or by Theodor Monod, still travelling the Mauritanian desert at 92, or the business and political heavyweights still active in their eighties, spectacularly exemplified by the American senator and Second World War veteran whose colleagues celebrated his hundredth birthday early in 2003. And what are we to think of the threat by Republican presidential candidate John McCain, 72, that he would send his mother, 95 and still vigorous, to wash the actor Chuck Norris's mouth out with soap for calling him 'too old' (February 2008)? Ageing is becoming a social phenomenon rather than a physical one; the violent cleavage of retirement, and the subsequent isolation, make people tired of life before their bodies are. It is no longer age that makes us old, but the world passing away from us. A time is approaching in which death will come following withdrawal from or distaste for a world that is no longer one's own; in which life will no longer be what is betrayed by the body, but what the mind abandons, betraying the body in the process. And everything depends on the plans society has for its elders; undoubtedly, everything depends on the usefulness it will acknowledge in them tomorrow; assuredly, everything depends even more on the capacity to act, in other words the autonomy and responsibility that it allows people to acquire. Training for long lifetimes, for the prolonged conversation of self with self, is becoming an imperative for tomorrow's Europe and America; so is each generation's assumption of responsibility for itself, the opposite of the alleged intergenerational solidarity that clothes the despoilment of future generations.

It is the young who face the real problem of ageing. The suicide rate among those aged 20–24 (12 per cent of deaths in that age group), higher than among the whole population, expresses the difficulty they have finding a place in a society that idealizes youth because it is withdrawing from it, and the better to withdraw from it. This is confirmed by a study conducted in 2007 by the HSBC to estimate the gap between people's expectations and the reality of their lives, analyzed by age group: in Britain as in France, dissatisfaction with life is greatest between 20 and 30 years of age, the highest level of satisfaction being found in the 55–65 group! The young are going to have to wait longer and try harder to find a role and a place that their elders are increasingly disinclined to yield to them. Is it by chance that in all the developed countries, an ever-increasing proportion of young people aged between 15 and 25 is regarded as unemployable, unable to function in the society of the market, contractual obligation and competition? Is it by chance that the spread of psychological disorders and dependencies has reached worrying proportions among the young in Europe, across all social levels and all origins?

Several lives in one

> She is a law student at Nanterre, working as a trainee in a lawyer's office in Bordeaux. 'I rent a room from my grandmother's boyfriend', she says, laughing. 'She's eighty, he's a bit younger, he must be seventy-two or seventy-five.'

The oneness of the body faced with a short lifespan and subject to state authority used to guarantee oneness of commitments. The explosion in life expectancy explodes those commitments. Marriage, as arranged and institutionalized in the nineteenth century, is the main victim of this situation. Saying 'I do', in church, temple or town hall, used to commit one for life; for an average of 15 or 20 years in 1900, although women generally married before 20; today, although the church or registry office comes ten years later, for more than 50 years on average. The same man or the same woman, for 50 years … will it still be the same bond after that time, the same relationship, the same gamble? 'Love only one and love her for ever', declares one of the heroes of *L'Éducation sentimentale*. We can envy those who live a love like that, or live on one; we can see it as the new ideal of a generation that discovered AIDS before discovering love. But how many are there who believe it possible, or even viable? Today's couples may say 'always', but it is not their word. Have not sexologists and psychologists identified conjugal fidelity as part of a fraught sexual pathology, and pointed out that (the number of sexual acts being closely linked to the number of sexual partners) conjugal commitment is contrary to the duty of well-being which is becoming our morality? Have not historians established that discourse on 'the eternal union of man and woman, mainstay of the family and society' refers to a very recent but already dated and constricting concept of the family? Apparently French men and women have understood this message. In urban environments, more than half of all marriages end in divorce or de facto separation. The average Frenchman in 2002 was more faithful to his bank than his wife, being able to stand it for longer: 16 years on average for the beloved, 22 on average for the bank. This last, however, is the average length of time spent as a couple by men and women, the longest ever known. When average life expectancy was under 30 years, it was difficult to live 20 years together.

Just as spectacular and problematic as the evolution of the conjugal bond is the confrontation of existing family and social models with the prolongation of sexually active youth into what used to be called the evening of life. All the more commonplace with the coexistence of five generations, from great-grandparents through to grandchildren, becoming frequent; all the more frequent because there is no longer a normal age to be sexually active, to make love, and to say so. Tradition, of course, no longer determines social roles by age; but the physical state of the body does not determine them either, especially as the gap is widening between social ages—sexual relations permitted between over-eighteens, but forbidden between an adult and a minor, retirement at 65—and physical ones—puberty having advanced by five years for girls and six for boys in a century, old age having receded by 20 or 30 years over the same period. Couples are forming at all ages, affecting the traditional forms of family life. These forms often contain little beyond memory or nostalgia in today's multiple families, with their overlapping generations; indeed they are fading into myth, all the more glowing and persuasive now that the reality of family relations, of the problematic cohabitations and surprising sexual promiscuities within clans a century or two ago, is less familiar and more idealized. It was not only in the Sicilian countryside that grandfathers begot children with their sons' wives, or in the Perche backwoods that girls were deflowered in a semi-public manner.

Reinventing roles

In this transformation of relations with time, lifespan and the major events of a life, what is more problematic is the disappearance here and there of structured, consistent forms of family life, whether family meals or holiday reunions; or even the major bonding celebrations that baptisms, weddings, communions and birthdays used to be, marking the stages of life while legitimizing and ordering them, and thus reducing the individual stress of deaths and mourning. The historically dated term 'family' is still used to designate amalgamations of interest in which thrift, taxation, sexuality, parenthood, mutual favours and services rendered maintain the contractual bond that passion or the amorous ideal do not maintain, and that belonging, earth and blood maintain no longer. Everyone must find his own role, for neither timetable, nor institution, nor society will do it for him now. More problematic, firstly, because the mixing of genders and roles can become sexually explosive. Is it just a coincidence that amid the current hysteria surrounding paedophilia, some people want to raise the minimum legal age for sexual relations between adults (admittedly to curb the new phenomenon in Europe of the forced marriages imposed on Muslim girls from the age of 15)? The disappearance of everyone's prescribed role, of the rituals that confirmed them, of the social forms that explained the family to outsiders, scrambles relationships, and growing ambiguity surrounds the withdrawn reserve of some clannish families in which several sexually active generations are living together. The accession of adolescents to maturity, which used to mark one of the high points of social life in earlier civilizations, is fudged and blurred by the loss of all landmarks.[2]

The relation between age groups no longer gives predetermined roles to everyone, either in the family or at work where the links between authority, knowledge, experience and age are no longer taken for granted; promotion by seniority will soon be as obsolete as pensioning people off at 55, and complaints of age discrimination are starting to be levelled at European businesses that exclude over-forties from training, and deny them promotion, as a matter of course. More problematic, moreover, because of the disappearance of the founding narratives, of the rituals of differentiation in which handing down or transmission used to take place, accumulating a shared collective unconscious where the rational and the emotional were brought together in a compulsory and exemplary pre-existing form. More problematic, but also more revealing of future modes of living, cross-generational and unpartitioned. If sensuality and sexuality were completely disconnected from procreation, from all competition, removed from the relationship market, would they turn the age of a

2. See on this subject Claude Alzon's essential work, *La Mort de Pygmalion—essai sur l'immaturité de la jeunesse*, Maspéro, 1974.

grandfather into the age of passion, of love at first sight, or simply of affection, of which the very young seem to be becoming incapable? The number of people of both sexes who think they have found and lived through reciprocated and satisfying amorous relationships in their fifties and sixties is rewriting the accepted scenario of amorous passion. Our Romeos and Juliets are past 60. With their parents dead and their children gone, their lives are their own. A few films and books have addressed the taboo subject of sexuality among senior citizens, our grandparents. The repression directed against it in so-called retirement homes, the embarrassment it causes among families and friends, have already given birth to original and innovative projects (often started by homosexual communities); these attitudes too can be expected to evolve given that loving, sensual relationships—sexualized or not—among senior and super-senior citizens are becoming ever more commonplace. After all, more than one Frenchman in three and one Frenchwoman in four say that they are sexually active beyond the age of 76. And is not the act of love a proven therapy against ageing?

Relations between the generations, in the family as in the workplace or holiday resort, are being modified by everyone's promiscuous exposure to the sexual activity of three or even four generations, where the traditional family with its three generations viewed as legitimate the sexuality of one generation only (that of the parents). Very few youngsters and young adults remain unaffected, in one way or another, when the flowering of new conjugalities among over-sixties underlines their own difficulties in starting their own relationships and organizing their lives. In 2005, advertising broke a taboo by showing a beautiful 55-year-old woman, sensual and desirable, saying: 'I'm in love.' Should we expect the new disorder in love relations to be caused by seniors, when the open display of amorous passion by those in their sixties and seventies is itself a major social change?

Just as problematic, and sometimes dramatic, is the break separating society as it is going—and as it wants to be, at the stated rhythm of an acceleration of time, of a rapid turnover of knowledge and achievements, condemning to obsolescence in advance any idea of maturity as a mastery of skills—from the lives of the very old, forgotten by time and, increasingly often, by their fellows. The fifth age of life is far too long for too many, an endless corridor leading to death. What can be said to those very ancient men in care homes who have seen none of their nearest and dearest, children or grandchildren, in 20 years? To those who have no one but nurses and carers for family, nothing but television for company, nothing but death to look forward to? A growing number of French women and men ought to give very serious thought to what they are going to do after the age of 90 or even 100 (women especially). The answer is not obvious, given that the need of these super-seniors for acceptance, help and company no longer finds a ready response in the family circle fractured by the demands of work and geographical mobility. The answer becomes even less obvious given that the increasingly commonplace figure of, say, a 75-year-old son mourning his mother, who died on 30 December 2004 aged 101, overturns our standard picture of ages, roles and identities. If 'you only become yourself after your parents have died' (Henry de Montherlant), most of our contemporaries will spend their lives in a protracted adolescence, the protective veil of their parents' longevity shielding them from reality, from the rules and from death: from themselves.

The scale of the social problem consecutive to the phenomenon of extended lifespan is due less to its financial, social and medical consequences and the care structures it requires than to the ignorance that surrounds it, which is worth dispelling and which asks in summary: what are people good for, what use are they, past the age of 80 or 90? What collective recognition does our society suggest for those who are the pioneers of the very long lifespan? The economic prospects of societies in which services to the individual represent a growing proportion of overall activity are directly and increasingly influenced by ageing, especially when it is accompanied by moral isolation and loss of contact with the family. But they have no bearing on the meaning of a long life, which you have to live for yourself, by yourself and with yourself.

A new timescale

> Two records were beaten during the Toronto Marathon run on 28 September 2003, to the general indifference of sporting chroniclers. A Canadian of 72 named Whitlock set a new over-70 world record by running the marathon in under three hours—2 hours, 59 minutes, 10 seconds—although he admitted after finishing that he felt 'dead on my feet'. Not all that far behind was an American of Indian origin, Fauga Singh, with another world record in an age category not, to tell the truth, all that hotly contested—the over-nineties—by running the 42.195 kilometres in 5 hours

> 40 minutes. Mr Singh, 92, attributed his fitness to meditation in Sikh temples, a daily curry and a 16-kilometre walk or run every day.

How remote it seems, the time when women dressed in black and grey when they reached their fifties, preparing for imminent widowhood followed by an endless mulling-over of past life! Of course we know that tradition no longer determines everyone's role according to their age. What is new is that the body no longer determines it either. These days apprentice skiers, IT technicians or pilots in their sixties rub shoulders with perpetual students, precociously obese individuals and worn-out middle managers 20 or 30 years younger. The dissociation of age from learning or training is a characteristic phenomenon of metamorphoses in the mode of transmission, and it is one of the causes of the new difficulty in that transmission. How remote it seems, the time when Saint-Just turned the duty of burning incense on the altar of the Nation over to 'old men of sixty'! (*Les institutions de la République*, 1792). The physical state (curved spine, stiff joints, suspect heart, etc.) of those late eighteenth-century oldsters is today that of men over 75. Our Western humanity is on the verge of a new age, and our relationship with time will be changed by it: a threshold that opens onto the unknown.

In 1900, in a human lifetime, adolescence lasted from 11 to about 16, young adulthood from 16 to 22, adulthood from 22 to 40, and after that old age set in. Some conscripts in 1939 already had all the signs of precocious ageing; and what are we to say of those photographs taken in the 1920s of Breton peasants in their forties, looking like today's octogenarians?

By 1960, helped by the belated adoption of compulsory schooling for all until 16, adolescence had expanded somewhat in both directions—from 10 to 18—with young adulthood extending from 18 to 25 and adulthood continuing to the edge of retirement, from 25 to 60.

Moving forward, though, it is more than obvious that between 1980 and 2000 things became further scrambled in terms of several major landmarks:

—While adolescence still begins at around 10 to 14, or even earlier, but is prolonged until nearly 25 or 30, the youngest now copy the practices of their elders in all areas, including those most harmful to their future well-being.

—Young adults are adopting conventional behaviour (lasting

commitments, assumption of professional, social and family responsibilities) at a later age, between 30 and 45 or even 50, the age of definitive life choices being retarded by 20 years on average, an effect in part of the economic crisis of the early 1990s. The French film *Tanguy* illustrates an unexpected but commonplace situation; it is usual today to hear a man of 35 rejecting all commitment and responsibility, still living his life as an adolescent; the most significant marker of adulthood is the purchase of a washing machine, something many still lack at 30!

—Adults locate themselves by the lasting, and in many cases definitive, character of their life choices between the ages of 45 and 65–75, this delay in the assertion of self originating notably in the close company, or at the very least the increasingly persistent presence, of the parents' and even the grandparents' generations in the lifecycle; many in their forties now have a living grandparent; many couples in their fifties benefit from handouts or notarized gifts from their parents, and many past retirement age still have a living parent. The pivotal age, the one at which the major choices and major investments are finalized, at which life ceases to be an adventure, settled at around 30 at the beginning of the last century; today it is over 50, if indeed the idea still has a meaning.

—Old age—being tired of life and the body starting to fail irremediably in some of its vital functions—only starts after that, and sometimes not until well beyond 80 years. It is not very unusual to come across these very old people from another era, aged 90 or over, who are still free from the small and great miseries of old age.

—Conjugality is turned upside down by long life. Some few individuals may share their lives with the same person for 60, 70 or 80 years. More numerous henceforth will be men and women for whom each major stage of personal or professional life will correspond to the construction of a new life, in a new couple, all the way to the beginning of great old age, which may itself renew or create unexpected amorous bonds. It is apparent that the link between kinship—or descent—and communal life is loosening; having a child or children no longer necessarily means living with them; more determining and essential than the biological bond is responsibility for the children, economic and social responsibility, responsibility for moral and cultural upbringing; a bond that is taking its time to find

> adequate juridical and social forms. Observation of the course people's lives are now taking leads us to acknowledge modes of conjugality that are not so much new as newly recognized, emerging from the confusion of roles between couple, kinship and sexuality—source of so much damage, breakdown and loneliness—reinventing marriage as an institution and life commitment, and asserting the difference between conjugality and sexuality ... is sleeping together without going to bed together a modern figure for luxury and mutual pleasure?

The new ages of life

It isn't really that the stages of life have disappeared. The different physiological ages are still there; while puberty comes earlier than it did, for girls as well as boys, the menopause and andropause are still the thresholds they always were, except that they are becoming less uncomfortable. As if nothing had changed, the titles of magazines, of books dealing with human life, fashion or consumption continue to adopt as a primary criterion of segmentation the landmarks of childhood, adolescence, adulthood and retirement. Banks, retailers and marketing men, through idleness or herd instinct, do the same. But the timing of major life events is now enormously variable. Increasingly, men and women inhabit the stage of life they deserve to inhabit, the one they have chosen, the one they have constructed. But watch out for the bank that refuses credit to a sexagenarian who is starting a new family and moving house! Watch out for the age-related mark-up in insurance! And even more for age discrimination in the job market! Who is to say that age, or background, or gender, can have any bearing on performance, independently of the individual and their history? The stages already past are a closed book to the registry office. The socialized, statutory rhythms of life—legal majority, legal retirement age, etc.—are increasingly out of synch with personal rhythms that have become reversible, non-sequential, random: consumer's or borrower's or investor's rhythms. These landmarks are further scrambled by the fact that some of the biological factors regarded as most infallible are yielding to the rising tide of technology. The most determining of these, the frontier of fertility in women, has been defied successfully several times, by the efforts among others of an Italian doctor who specializes in helping women complete pregnancies at 60 years old, with some success. It is not by chance that Viagra is emblematic of the new frontiers being attacked by biology. The frontier between non-responsible child and responsible adult has probably dropped by three to four years over the last half-century, making it legitimate to judge and punish young miscreants of 13 or 14, who would have been guaranteed impunity under the old definition of childhood. And the most apparent frontier, the visible relaxation of muscles, the appearance of wrinkles, is under attack by vitamin supplements, HRT, botox or growth hormone which, at the trifling cost of a daily injection, can bring time's wingéd chariot to a sort of halt at the magical age of 25. This suggests that if long lifespans promise in the end to change the structure of consumption, it is not because seniors no longer consume or invest, but because they consume and invest differently.

However schematic it may be, this presentation is nearer the mark than the one, based on received ideas and intuition, that suggests the lengthening of lifespan prolongs the duration of old age, in other words the duration of physical suffering, of letting oneself go, of the shipwreck that De Gaulle believed he could see in all old age ("Old age is a shipwreck", in *Mémoires d'Espoir*, 1970–71). The months of life gained with every year that passes are months of life in good health; there is even an observable shortening tendency in the period marked by more or less profound dependence (living to a greater age is less important than the shortening of this period of dependence: 12 months in 1970, 9 months in 2005), marked too by the disability or mental disorders that used to precede the end of life (the prevention of Parkinsonism and Alzheimer's disease would mark an important stage in that effort). Even though the statistical extension of life expectancy is more spectacular at 60 than it is at 20 (owing to relatively high mortality from accidents and risky personal conduct among young adults), the extension is due less to very old people dragging out the burden of living for another year or two than to sprightly retired folk prolonging their years of active and enjoyable living. This phenomenon can be read more easily in recent studies on the physical condition of senior citizens than in mortality tables: a man of 75 today is in the same physical state as his grandfather would have been at 60. We do not live longer old and sick, we live longer as adults without feeling age except through moral weakness, inactivity or disarray. Unemployment, public assistance or idleness age people who would be kept young, with an undiminished appetite for life, for their normal span, by work, love or passion, and above all by the wish to be attractive. All the phases of life are overturned by the phenomenon of long lifespan—so that the traditional typology of the ages following one another at known and unavoidable intervals in the lives of people in general has become false. The succession of the ages of life is no longer sequential, dictated by the passage of time. The link between age, body and lifestyle is less immediate than ever before; this is a new margin of freedom given to all; to choose one's age, or at least to live the age one chooses. Available life choices have greatly diversified at every age, partly because the direct and disabling aspects of old age are appearing later, even in some cases not appearing at all. How many men and women are there now who will retain to their dying day an appetite for knowledge, for activity, for relations with others, and for feeling useful: who are still good for something?

Choosing one's age

> In November 2007 Arielle Dombasle, cohabiting partner of the author Bernard-Henry Lévy, was performing in the Crazy Horse Saloon in Paris as a leading chorus girl at the age of 54. In 2008 the Portuguese film-maker Manoel de Oliveira showed his 47th film at the Venice [festival], at the age of 99, and Valerie Ramsay, 67, was a star model with the San Francisco-based Look Talent Agency.

Are we on the threshold of the end to ageing, that dream of endless generations? Even before European law makes it impossible to evade a few of the consequences in terms of work contracts, it is already becoming less possible to label an individual as young, adult or elderly strictly according to registry office data, for it is less a matter of figures limiting the stages of life, as it used to be in the days of short lifespan, than of personal choice. Europeans are going to be the age they choose to be; that is the implicit promise of a European law forbidding all discrimination in matters of pay, responsibility or promotion on the basis of age (Directive of 2002 on employment) rather than strictly individual performance criteria. What indicates old age is now the absence of a life plan, not the number of years lived. It is as if, depending on their professional, sentimental and financial situation, depending on their appetite for life and their vision of their bodies, our contemporaries may choose the age they want to have and place themselves at will in one stage of life or another. A Dr de Jaeger, who specializes in treating precocious ageing, neatly summed this up by quoting a phrase used by one of his clients: 'when I was old...' (*Science Revue*, February 2003). Professor Yves Christen, President of the Ipsen Foundation, observes that 'consent to growing old ... is more wearing than age itself'.

'I started to live well and kick over the traces at 48, free from family, money and career worries...'. The real experience of a resurgence of youth, of passion, of desire, characterizes the life courses of adults or senior citizens not because they can arrest the course of time, but because they are ready for several lives. The impossible resurgence of youth is no longer just the mythological fantasy it has always been; and if it now seems a possibility it is not just a matter of elixirs, Viagra, Botox or HRT, but more as if being young were less a matter of age, a mechanical effect of the calendar and the passage of time on the body, and more a matter of choice or taste, an effect of individual will, achieved through the enlightened mediation of medicine, psychology, dietetics and fashion. Parents of married children play the adolescent, take part in the Sunday-night roller rallies through the Paris streets, escape the everyday in wild nights at holiday clubs, and dream at 50 or 60 that life is just beginning. The book published in 2002 under the expressive title *Les adulescents* provides examples of a phenomenon whose manifestations touch everyone, but without assessing its significance. As if the French were emancipating themselves in large part from the registry of births, marriages and deaths to live at the age they decide for themselves. This unheard-of plasticity is simultaneously a manifest illusion, an explosive promise and a source of well-being (or intense frustration), and any move to question it seems unthinkable. Seen from this angle, what is at issue is clearly a conquest, a fait accompli. To question it would not be to reverse it; and after it, there can be no question of going back to the way things were.

Abundance

Obesity looks like it is becoming the sickness of the century. Half a million deaths a year are attributed to it in the US, and 50,000 a year are already linked to excess body weight in France. Fifty million Americans are affected by obesity (defined by a body mass index over 30, the index being obtained by dividing the person's weight in kilograms by their height in metres squared) in their life expectancy and physical capacities. Nearly half of all Americans are overweight. Obesity, the combined result of bad diet, stress and physical inactivity, will in the years to come overtake tobacco to

> become the first cause of mortality, and will be a pitiless social marker: eating well means dieting now. Water-borne infections (cholera and dysentery) and the pathologies caused by malnutrition and unhealthy housing used to make the poor die young and keep natural selection going; obesity is set to perform the same role by making the poor die before their time.

After the longer lifespan comes abundance. Abundance of money, and the improbable privilege of detachment it provides, the privilege of the West. Wealth, with the overabundance of products it offers, with their threat to exhaust our desire and stifle any possible satisfaction.

Despite the rapid ascent of China and India, in 2008 less than 20 per cent of the world population produces 60 per cent of world output. Less than 10 per cent of the world population owns 80 per cent of world financial wealth. And less than 2 per cent owns nearly half of it. All split, with very few exceptions, between the US (how widely known is it that Florida is the world's second richest state after the US?), Europe and Japan. Taking into account public policies, the multiplication of free services and unconditional handouts, no part of the world at any time in history has offered such luxurious living conditions, security and freedom, almost without return in terms of work or commitment, than the countries of Western Europe over the last 50 years. But for how much longer?

Wealth and mobility

This concentration of abundance and productive activity has not appeared by accident but is the fruit of a revolution, political rather than economic, that gave a hitherto inconceivable force to the private contract, across frontiers, that made liquid and fluid what used to be rooted and connected, and that is establishing property rights over what has never before been the object of private appropriation: life, genes, living matter. Laws ratifying entrepreneurial conquests used to be the determining factor in wealth creation; the appropriation of living tissue is becoming the new motor of private enrichment.

Despite the pessimistic forecasts of economists like Marx and Schumpeter in predicting—for very different reasons—the exhaustion of capitalism and the entrepreneurial spirit, the 1980s and 1990s saw the free-enterprise countries achieving considerable and unexpected advances for themselves, and moving towards making abundance and market access universally available. While the physiognomy of wealth distribution will doubtless be very different in the decade between 2020 and 2030—by which time Europe and the US could see their relative share halved to the profit essentially of China and India—it will really be because the space of private property and free enterprise will have spread across the world. Despite wars and revolutions—and sometimes because of them—Europe has conserved into the beginning of the twenty-first century the essence of what its initiatives, conquests and innovations have earned it: its structural capital. The effect of this exceptional structural capital can be seen in one figure: the productivity per hour of a French office worker in 2004 was one of the world's highest, ahead of American productivity, far ahead of German or British, and five to ten times higher than that of a Chinese, an Indian or a South African.[3]

The world's wealth used to be patrimonial; now it is linked to the circulation of money, services and information, and participation in the global growth movement is continuously being extended into new territories, and within those territories into more layers of the population. Local cultures are steadily losing ground to cash-register cultures. Mobility makes the wealth that rootedness makes no longer. We have reached the point where luxury brands have to manage mass markets; also and more importantly, the point where piloting the industrial-scale production and distribution of products that retain the flavour and appeal of handmade quality for the consumer, positioning and promoting the experience of brands chosen for their exclusivity by the mass of customers, in regional or global markets, is the challenge that justifies the investment of empires like LVMH (Moët-Hennessy Louis Vuitton) or PPR (a French multinational specializing in luxury retail) in the big names of fashion, perfume, leather goods or lifestyle. Car makers, luxury goods craftsmen, furniture makers and fashion houses, yacht and luxury house builders were all confronted during the 1990s by this once-improbable situation: a shortage of goods expensive enough to satisfy their customers. The price explosion for exclusive products measures the private wealth and demand for

3. Where an American worker produces 100 units in an hour, the French worker produces 106.6, the German 91.7 and the Briton 78.6; a Japanese, only 67.5; although the gap in purchasing power favours the American worker by 25 per cent, the greater number of hours worked and greater number of years in a working life explain the difference *in fine*. Source: Patrick Artus and Gilbert Cette, *Eurostat, and [CAE] report on productivity and growth*, May 2004.

distinction of the 'super-rich' (individuals with a personal worth of $100 million or more); the explosion that now has cars on the market at several hundred thousand euros (more than a million in the case of the VAG-manufactured Bugatti Veyron), that has the prices paid for desirable residences skyrocketing, that leads some brands (like Louis Vuitton in its Paris shop) to restrict the number of articles a customer can buy, illustrates a tendency without historical precedent—the permanent emancipation of a significant part of Western, and increasingly Asian, populations from the experience of scarcity, and thus from thrift as it used to be, from what money used to cost to get, from the bank and its penny-pinching. It seems that the 2007–09 crisis had little impact on the rapid increase in the number of very large individual fortunes in India, China and elsewhere; in Asia, sales of luxury products led the post-crisis recovery.

Earners in retirement

Compared to other parts of the world, where old age is still a curse with destitution close on its heels, and compared to the US—where the progressive abandonment of 'defined benefit' systems (in which the company contributing for its staff guarantees the size of their future pensions, a commitment that almost bankrupted General Motors) in favour of 'defined contribution' systems (in which the company only undertakes to contribute a defined sum) makes the level of retirement pensions dependent on the health of financial markets—Europe guarantees an unheard-of level of comfort to its retired, but one that cannot endure. Over half a century marked by a general tendency for Europeans to become richer, the growth of purchasing power and property ownership among the retired is even more striking than among the population at large. The ruin and destitution of retirement and pensions in 1944 was succeeded by what can only be called a golden age of retirement. Abundance of resources combined with the fullness of time. A retired couple who have both completed a full career today enjoy a standard of living no previous generation has ever obtained, from pensions needed for two or three times as long as they were by earlier generations (especially in the case of women, who benefit from a pension reversion policy when they outlive older husbands); and this situation will become more frequent as couples in which the wife was 20 years old during the 1960s, when full-time work for women became widespread, claim their retirement rights. A strange deficiency of perspective explains this situation. Debate has always been focused on the monthly income available to retired people, never on the total purchasing power distributed to them during their retirement; and while the first of these has merely grown at the same rate as salaries, the second has exploded over the last 30 years, the increase in life expectancy helping, so that a retired couple having claimed their pensions in 1980 will receive an amount more than three times that paid to their parents who retired in 1956 (estimated in constant-value francs, then euros, inflation factored out)!

The effects of this gigantic redistribution are plain to see. Organized tours, cruises, luxury blocks, Michelin-starred restaurants are crammed with the over-sixties who benefit from it. The over-sixties in France own three times as many stocks and shares as under-forties; they have benefited from the re-balancing of capital earnings against salary earnings (in 2004 the Total oil company paid its shareholders a sum equivalent to its annual wages and salary bill!). Between 1945 and 2000, the purchasing power of a pensioner was multiplied more than sixfold; that of a wage or salary earner 'only' quadrupled. And this retired people's purchasing power is transforming the market of services to the individual, creating micro-property markets, as in general it is adding to the pressure on housing apparent in a coastal band 20 to 50 kilometres wide, running from Normandy to the Côte d'Azur. France's blue belt is a grey belt too. Old people's homes, on the model of Paradiseland or a Disney World for the elderly, some of whose hidden workings are exposed in the book *Leisureville* (2008), have proliferated along the Florida coast.

A conservation society

Old age has been freed from want. Throughout the European Union, ceasing to work, retirement and old age are no longer signs of poverty, not even of dependence on children or relations; the extraordinary thing is not that this advance has been accomplished in less than 50 years, it is that the situation of pensioners is these days seen as a right, and the maintenance or even the increase of their purchasing power as an absolute political imperative. For the scale of replacement incomes (the ratio between the pension amount and the salary level just before retirement) elsewhere, including Japan and the US, is nowhere near the European level, and there are a lot of countries, China and Russia among them, where stopping work means destitution for anyone lacking family support. Such a leap in pensioners' incomes has no equivalent at any point in history in any other society, especially as it is accompanied by extensive guarantees; guaranteed incomes, in societies to which the market extends the dominion of volatility and chance: that is what is really exceptional. It indicates the limits of the solidarity so often cited by those who benefit from it; solidarity in claiming their share of the benefits, not of the risks. It announces that the nineteenth-century opposition between rich and poor will be succeeded in the twenty-first by a conflict between those who live from their labour and those who live from social handouts and redistribution. The first signs of this are already apparent, most notably in the debates on a strong euro and price stability which favour pensioners, structurally in credit, at the expense of young people who are structurally indebted. And it is catching us unprepared. Wealth creation does not make a society; not any more, or not on this side of the Atlantic—the opposite of the American situation where the hope of acquiring wealth is an active and powerful catalyst for integration, and where wealth earned through work and merit keeps the forge of integration white-hot. 'Wealth', or more exactly the standard of living and quality of life that are rather glibly associated with it, does not signify that there has been any advance in the integration of the elderly into European or French society. Sometimes they mean the opposite, as the deaths of isolated elderly people during the heat wave in the summer of 2003 cruelly showed, and sometimes to a point where the isolation of grandparents and great-grandparents, in the absence of recognition and personal bonds, seems to be in exact proportion with the social incomes they are granted, as if society were getting rid of its old people at the cost of the public purse, in keeping with the time-honoured propensity of public money to make unhappy those who believe it to be a blessing.

A conservation society is taking shape, in the name of an absolute preference for survival. For such an increase in old people's incomes marks a major distortion of the relation between the elderly and the active young, to the advantage of the elderly, as well as the one between earned income and disposable income, especially as the free time available to the retired produces an income effect that can be estimated at 15 to 20 per cent of supplementary real purchasing power compared to that of an active earner (access to leisure activities at cut prices, freedom to attend sales during working hours, time to 'shop around', etc.). Senior citizens have unparalleled access to price concessions and grants of all sorts. A lot of services are provided free, including healthcare, whose real cost increases at a rate the square of age (under-25s cost health insurance less than 100 euros a year, while over-85s cost 5,000 euros a year)… Young pensioners in good health, the beneficiaries of full employment in their early working lives, then of the financial and share boom, have revenue requirements out of proportion with those of their children who are subject to insecure employment, have sometimes had to weather stock-market crashes, and are financially dependent on their parents and grandparents to an extent unknown in the past. This gap in revenue requirements will grow still further with the massive arrival of the baby boom generations at retirement age, from 2005 to 2020: populous generations, aware of their interests and intransigent on their rights, including many who quite simply expect a pension equal to their working salary, some even getting it despite the manifestly unaffordable nature of such a demand. The subject of guaranteed incomes for senior citizens, on a compulsory basis, is facing the Western countries. The pensions question lies before us. Not as we would want it to be; like the reverse of the way our societies accommodate the active young.

This question deserves to be clarified with an observation that economists and labour sociologists have been reiterating for years, at least since the European countries as a whole undertook to allow for lengthening life expectancy by delaying the legal retirement age (in France, under the Balladur reform of 1995 and the Fillon law of August 2003): that labour productivity does not diminish with age, contrary to the apparently self-evident general view.[4] Conflict is breaking out here between the body and the law. Very destructive in France is the combination of two absurdities: a defined legal retirement age, and the even more absurd business practice of getting rid of staff members over 50 (of course, the wish to let older staff go has to do with the established link between salary levels and seniority, and with the social constraints involved in sacking people over 50: the law condemns those it purports to protect). So-called 'masters' (staff aged 50 plus) and 'seniors' (staff aged 60 and over) have a considerable capacity for creating value, in large part because their availability and concentration are greater than those of younger workers whose shoulders carry all sorts of burdens—family, child-raising, career, etc.—subjecting them

4. See notably Patrick Aubert and Bruno Crépon, 'Travailleurs salariés et l'emploi', in *Économie et Statistiques*, No. 368, INSEE.

between the ages of 25 and 40 to an improbable and gruelling commando obstacle course (with a 25 per cent unemployment rate among under-25s, and being the country that puts its youth to work later than any other in the world, and later forces them into retirement earlier than anyone else, France is aggravating a source of tension that plays a large part in feeding collective anxiety).

Signposts that need inventing

Personal enrichment as a means to well-being—perhaps more concretely satisfaction or contentment—leads to a certain disconnection. Money buys indecisiveness, it liquidates memberships, identities, origins, undertakings and age itself. It fabricates youth and buys time; that at least is what the economy of the body promises, with obsessive insistence and fallacious complacency. Whether applied to dietary, sexual, sartorial or professional choices, the principles of satisfaction and contentment empty of all meaning the once-widespread logics of restraint, sacrifice and punishment. Family and social roles are changed, especially as this promise for the first time is made to women along with men. And their effects on work, enterprise and consumption have still hardly been glimpsed, so thoroughly have they overturned previous models. We have to get used to the fact that grandparents devoted to their grandchildren may also be sexually active, seducers or flirts, with the financial means for it as well as—perhaps more than—the physical means, spending money to assert attractiveness, and to maintain or revive their physical capacities. We have to get used to the fact that the holders of the family property may also be demanding consumers of travel, leisure activity, sports and culture along with various pleasures, and that age has nothing to do with the extent of these pleasures and life-experiences, or with their intensity, constantly being raised to hitherto unknown thresholds. The time when panels of cosmetics and beauty product consumers included no one over 65 will soon seem remote. As if the wish to attract and the image of self simply ceased on the threshold of a contracting old age, except in the schematic frame of marketing studies! There is a gold mine awaiting health and well-being industrialists who can offer people over 65 or 70 the right products for their living conditions and their physical and moral state; for age increases beyond measure the premium payable for guaranteed well-being, maintenance of lifestyle and preservation of self-image.

What counts though is not so much the revenue side as the consumption side. Images of the West as perceived in Hanoi, Antananarivo or Ulan Bator are of groaning shelves, resplendent display windows and the superabundance of material goods; images of merchandise, of its reign, its triumph. Even the offhand waste of merchandise plays a part in this myth of the civilization of superabundance. These images are powerfully validated by the obsession with the consumer that haunts our own societies: how to arouse his desire, how to reawaken his desire, how to ensure that he stays unsatisfied, hounded by insatiable longings? Satisfaction has stopped being the objective of our societies and become their worst-case scenario; to keep selling, and thus producing more, you need unsatisfied consumers. Their desire had to be aroused; now its insatiability has to be ensured. Perpetually unsatisfied obsessives, bulimics, are the ideal consumer citizens required for growth. The metamorphosis of bulimic consumer of products into demanding giver of orders for services is one of the faces of the transformation of Western societies.

Even though its spectre continues to feed collective fears and to haunt the self-serving chronicle of public debate, poverty is now only a relative economic problem in our developed societies, and will soon become a figure purged of want and need, necessary only as a negative image, to highlight distance and distinction. A relative economic problem, but a social and political problem of the greatest importance: the problem of damaged self-esteem, the problem of isolation, of psychic and moral disarray which has as a consequence (rather than a cause) a tendency to fall into precarious and dramatic individual financial situations. If there is a vital economic problem it is the opposite one of overconsumption, bulimic absorption of material goods, backed by the permanent need for such overconsumption to feed growth; how many more people die from overeating and overconsumption in our gorged societies than ever died in former times from extreme destitution? Even in Brazil obesity is a growing national curse, already more than apparent on Copacabana beach. Millions of American consumers are paying and will pay in extra kilos, in their pathological bulimia, in their frenetic shopping, for the fact that the mythical character they comprise—'the American consumer'—rescued the world economy during the great Argentinean and Russian financial crisis. So that now the old curses of work, hunger and suffering have ceased to affect the West; so that new horizons of choice lie open under our once incredulous, now blasé gaze. How much has private prosperity done to thrust back, along with the spectre of want, the world's enchantment: those practices of magic, of the gift, of the collective dream, that used to transmute shared poverty into supernatural wealth? With more analysts and psychiatrists than physicians in Paris's fifth arrondissement, the face of uncertainty, of anxiety, of distress and self-doubt, is becoming the downside of abundance, and the dominant collective feeling of societies that no longer know how they are constituted, now that they are not the collective form of survival.

This is an unprecedented situation. A majority of Europeans have more means than projects: where they are poor is in appetite for life, confidence and self-esteem rather than cash or property. It is a long time now since competing companies realized that they needed to produce a lot more desire than services or goods, that what they had to produce from now on was unfulfilment; unless they wanted to see their markets dry up, the material needs of their customers quickly saturated, their desires assuaged ... their appetite gone. Producing desire is the primary trade of competing businesses, one that counts far more than ensuring the quality of the products or services that will be used in real life by consumers drowning in value and functionality. The link between our unprecedented prosperity and the disenchantment of the world ought to be exposed in this harsh light. The sated stomach shuts both eyes and both ears to the God who watches over all.

A state of peace

> Guadalcanal may be the turning point of this war. But it'll cost lives, Stavros. Is that what's bothering you? I've explained to you the importance of this objective. How many men do you think it's worth? How many lives?
>
> from the film *The Thin Red Line* (dir. Terrence Malick)

At last, the reign of peace. Without it, no long life; without it, no really beneficial enrichment, none of the tranquillity of mind and body brought by the certainty of lacking nothing, and the equally comforting certainty of risking nothing. Decades have passed since anyone in Europe has had to wonder how many deaths an objective would cost; or how many individual lives would have to be sacrificed to keep Europe alive. Several decades too since the objective of 'zero casualties' has guided the operational tactics of American intervention forces, most recently in Afghanistan,

Iraq and elsewhere, accelerating the privatization of warfare. Who is to decide who lives, and who dies? The supreme values used to be the ones you could kill for, or die for; when the supreme value becomes not killing and not dying, the models change. All our values have life as their limit. The whole of Europe takes it for granted that nothing is worth more than a life, and sees this attitude as denoting a higher level of civilization.

Peace, or rather the illusion of the world's goodness, of history stopping, of the reconciliation of all with all and for ever, make the illusion of 'zero risk' possible and revive the illusion of mastering time, manifest behind the rise of the precautionary principle, its generalization and the fact that it is required. How can we accept that such disparate catastrophes —Bhopal, Seveso, Chernobyl, BSE and its pyres, the explosion of the AZF factory in Toulouse, shipwrecks like the *Erika* or the *Prestige*—can arise from peace, when the very idea of war appears distant? It is not just war that ought to disappear, but death too; and incidentally, Europe has made its abolition of the death penalty a symbol of its wish for peace. Or rather that with the disappearance of war every vital threat—like the chance of death or unexpected weather—is perceived in an exaggerated fashion as a threat to survival, awakening reflexes of self-defence, wariness or flight.

The time has passed when every statesman was defined primarily by his posture in time of war, an acid test that destroyed some and consecrated others. Thiers, Gambetta, Clémenceau, De Gaulle… Europe's great men, in their great majority, have been men at war, even though not all were warlike men. We have to forget all of that (but for how long?). The possibility of war's reappearance in Europe, in former Yugoslavia, against Islamist terrorism, against the potential invasion that threatens a demographically disarming continent, has been carefully censored out of public debate and officially sanctioned opinion to avoid troubling the serenity of the consumer and saver. The assertion of power by Islamic communities, which is currently turning Holland upside down causing a significant exodus of ethnic Dutch nationals, and is already more than apparent in some big French, British and German cities, is being ignored to avoid confronting it.[5] With its naïve, somewhat forced faith in established peace, the European Union is parting company with the rest of the world, which still knows what force of arms and the edge of a sword can mean as promise or

5. See David Pryce-Jones, 'Europe's "Terrible Transformation"', *Commentary*, July–August 2007.

guarantee. In Europe—should that be only in Europe?—the body is no longer state property, corporal punishment has disappeared from the schools, and mass call-up has vanished over the horizon along with universal conscription.

The dream of withdrawal

Progress is manifest, but equally apparent is a process of withdrawal into the protective cell of individual, professional or family life. When peace appears to be definitively established, that process can continue without the obvious existence of risk, and vital risk, focusing our attention on the part played by the collective, by power, and by the link between them, in the quality of life we enjoy. It seems to go without saying that henceforth, nothing can come between oneself and humanity; is the dismissal—still more symbolic than real—of all communal membership, whether of origin, religion, language or territory, really a means to peace, or is it the way to a new barbarism? And is the guarantor of peace to be some rational, mobile, rootless idiot, whose sole concern is to maximize his personal advantage in terms of the attractiveness of different territories? Examination of that inconsistent but omnipresent figure would compel us to overturn the consensus view that peace has become the immovable, permanent state of our societies, and stop reducing the political to the social, and the social to the defence of social subsidies. The very idea of the sacrifice of the individual to the community, to something bigger than a single life, has been systematically denigrated and emptied of meaning; the suppression of the death penalty, and the hysteria that surrounds the very idea of capital punishment in Europe, illustrate this hope that we can sidestep adversity by denying evil.

Anyone who has witnessed—in Beirut in the 1970s and 1980s, in Israel during the Iraqi invasion of Kuwait, and later during the American intervention in Iraq—the scrum of panic buyers seeking sugar, oil, rice, mineral water, petrol and so on, knows how worthless is wealth consisting only of money, and that real wealth starts with confidence in tomorrow. What strength there is in the commonplace remark: 'It's being delivered tomorrow'! If deliveries of heating oil, petroleum, gas, bread or electricity are being compromised or are interrupted, if a transport strike threatens freedom of movement and access to public transport, regarded as a right, what vertigo must result in our just-in-time, zero-stocks, 24-hour-delivery societies! The management of businesses, the capillarity of systems for distribution, subcontracting and outsourcing, as well as the running of large-scale facilities for the health and security of populations, presuppose established peace, in much the same way that the social mothering to which the institutions, the state, the religions and politics have been reduced excludes the possibility of any confrontation, internal or external. War may not have been removed from the field of the possible, but for Europe and Europeans—and doubtless only for them—it has been excluded from the field of the thinkable.

An underlying illusion

This illusion of established abundance sheltered from the outside world took root in Western Europe, forgetful of the price of the US umbrella over nearly half a century, as the threat of Soviet tanks and aggression by Warsaw Pact forces against NATO became less immediate. To such a point that in 2003 (as in 2008 and 2009, when a gold bar was valued at over 20,000 euros) there were economists who expressed surprise at the massive flight from unrealized property values into precious stones, gold and other barbarous relics, having forgotten what the murmur of war outside the city walls can awaken in the collective unconscious. The illusory Western victory over the Soviet Union, the even more illusory war on terrorism and war on drugs (and soon, no doubt, the war on evil), have established the dangerous idea of a war without death, zero risk, the end of history; the idea of a Western sanctuary. The illusion of established peace transforms the societies it disarms; it is the precondition for the advent of the body. It was war that used to gather bodies together, to deliver bodies and lives to states, churches and ideologies, those cold, all-devouring monsters. It was war that used bodies as means to some absolute end: land, frontier, nation. Peace gives bodies back to themselves, to their pleasures, their well-being. The end of war marks an unprecedented liberation of bodies, a new conquest, a reunion with self-confidence. It also opens up new territories—aggression turned inwards, war on the self—and it clears the way for the advent of the body, which nothing foreign can threaten now.

Really this conviction is less a recognition of what is than the expression of a wish so common and so widely shared that it masks reality, or aspires to replace it. In international strategy, the notion of peace or war has no more reality these days than that of friendly or enemy countries; since the Second World War, wars are no longer declared, so that a state of war is seen as the final effect of a deterioration, on the slippery margins of an official state of peace. The battlefield no longer exists, since US nuclear deterrence and superpower have forbidden all localized conflict between states; but General Aidid booted the US Marines out of Somalia by getting ten-year-old children to carry his messages. The transformation of war has been such that the military are now far less threatened by it than civilians (in a little over a century, the proportion of military casualties in the total count dropped from 70 per cent during the Franco-Prussian war of 1870 to less than 20 per cent in Vietnam, Afghanistan, Chechnya and Sudan, and under 5 per cent in the wars in Sierra Leone and the Eastern Congo!). What with subversives, mafias and fanatics, enemies no longer have the texture of a state, or that of a clear target; they are among us. The zero-deaths objective is less a quest for peace than a demand for a radical separation of the peaceful world we want from the world in which others make war, and failing that—for it is impossible—a demand for the disappearance of the world. How stubbornly different it remains, how hostile it is, how bloated with open and concealed menace! If only it could disappear as a world and make way for a peace founded on contracts, unslaked desires and pre-formatted opinions; if only the world could be a market, if only the world could be one, if only it could be united, if only it could be the world no longer.

Peace as liberation

The central figure of peace at all costs, crucial to the advent of the body, is the statue erected to Life in place of everything else: the law, religious faith, all values, all freedoms. It authorizes aspiration to the sort of well-being that the pursuit of growth requires; it enables the advent of the body to become the advent of desire, and the body to become a perpetual desiring machine. And it inflects the advent of the body with the unrecognized advent of the woman's body, by stripping men of the dubious privileges of giving their lives for their country and killing their foes; the male privileges. With those privileges, some of the conditions for male supremacy fade, and the woman's authority over the details of life may extend to the state and transform the content of public policy. It permits the fragmentation of groups whose primary function was defensive, and the sidelining of the intermediaries who organized them and transmitted the memory of past conflicts, the survival knowledge and the will to endure. By unbinding individuals from the obligation to survive together by force of arms, it enables them to regroup in unprecedented, random, agile fashion, by musical or sartorial preference, by signs of other sorts: tribally, without a sacred dimension. It places the figure of peace among the collective beliefs, the necessary beliefs; and, to the point of casting doubt on Europe's capacity to maintain and apply its own laws, passes for a rebellious attitude and arouses the same censure that used to be focused on the body, pleasure and sex; country of origin becoming what sex used to be in the last century, that which it is forbidden to show and say. It postulates unanimity on the new articles of its public morality, which are called openness, universality, tolerance, but could equally well be called censorship, denial of reality and uniform thought. It is the measure of the absence of collective will, and even of a wish that no collective will should emerge to upset the individual comfort in which everyone can wallow in their own preferences and the dialogue of self with self; since it suggests that to ensure peace, all we need to do is pretend to have chosen everything that happens and live with it; it's just a matter of paying.

Preference for the body had security as its precondition: security for the self, for its property, its life; we are desperate to believe it is permanently established, without seeing clearly enough that some of the conditions for security, conditions that made the advent of the body possible, are being eroded by new threats (the end of nature, the appropriation of living tissue, the decline of frontiers). Progress in the privatization of the body had as its precondition the end of war, meaning the end of the body's subjection to the political order, the Nation's summons. We think we have seen the last of all that, without seeing clearly enough that peace is no longer an institutional state, but the effect of a superior capacity to act: the capacity to prefer ourselves, to be distinct from others and to be separate, that is now in question.

A body to be enjoyed

What is this body for, and this life? For enjoyment, of course. 'There's nothing wrong with doing yourself some good', sang Dany, dark-haired muse of the '70s Parisian night. Just so; indeed we should go further and mention the duty of pleasure, the obligation to enjoy oneself, formulated in the literature of personal development that marks the third age of the

> narrative: after the epic that founded the community, after the ballad and the novel, those motors of individuation, come the books of personal development to serve the new order of well-being as the abyss in which to collapse into oneself. 'Fear of Missing Out syndrome' is the emblematic symptom of what now passes for living a good life: it is no longer a matter of applying God's law on earth, ensuring human progress or bypassing history, more a matter of accumulating experiences. In the shadow of Sydney's expressionist Opera House, as in rebuilt Beirut, the city's biggest library devotes its largest section to all the ways of doing yourself some good, from personal development to health cookery and relaxing massages as recommended by Tibetan mystics.

For the first time, in a West hitherto subject to the confrontation between good and evil, body and soul, eternity and the passing moment, a good life is a life devoted to pleasure.[6] Being a good person these days does not mean curbing the sinful longings of the body, mortifying the weak flesh, following your conscience and preparing through constant prayer for your departure from this life here below; it means living well. Bad cess to anyone who lets a day pass without some enjoyment! Love, sports, booze, chatting or dining with friends; the libraries of personal development repeat in a competitive litany that to get on well with others, at home, at work, you have first to get on well with yourself. For centuries people deplored egotists who thought first of themselves, and condemned pleasure-seeking behaviour. We are far removed from that, so far that 'sex' signifies pleasure instead of difference, so far that the outstanding images of recent years, from the Lectures on Undressing given at Galeries Lafayette on boulevard Haussmann on Thursday afternoons in 2004 to Aubade's 'Seduction lessons', are images of the body as a promise, as a pleasure and a game; so far that great French chefs are seen as modern heroes, whose victories arrive on plates, not on the battlefield; so far that Anita Pallenberg, Marianne Faithfull and Catherine Millet pass for modern saints, having given so much to those who so needed them; when the body is in power, what gift could be more precious, more coveted and more meritorious than the gift of one's body? The body has changed less than the gaze brought to bear on it. What was once doomed to suffer, deserve and forgive is doomed now to enjoy, endure and forget.

---

6. For a view of the recurrent debates on this subject, see Dale Martin's book on the quarrel between Corinthian Christians concerning the relation with the body and with pleasure, *The Corinthian Body*, Yale University Press, 1999.

The good life

When the Marquis de Sade's characters parade their sole concern—to do themselves some good—their avowals and the demonstrations they concoct around their delectable prey have the force of blasphemy; and the pious Justine remains forever associated with that. The young business executive, the young woman consultant, who summarize their weekend by saying 'I had a good time', or 'I went completely potty at the sales', have the innocence of a confession of the obvious; both are on earth to have a good time. Not to perform dazzling acts or aspire to heroism, not to occupy the place assigned to them by a higher order, not even to accumulate and pass on; just to get the most they can out of it. Recalling the Saturday shopping and its radical impact on the credit card, the evening with friends, the Sunday devoted to a long, health-restoring bike ride, they have little idea of the abrupt abandonment, in less than two generations, of the world of dues and bonds for the world of the self and rights. The real revolution is the one that has given everyone a taste of the privilege enjoyed by yesterday's aristocrat: his own pleasure, and nothing more. What is a lifetime that is not devoted to pleasure really worth?

The good life is the one you fancy. And the one your body fancies. But that body is a newborn one, new in the sense that it is promised to pleasure before being dedicated to the state or the lord, through war service, to the community or enterprise, through labour, to reproduction or even to simple individual survival. And its advent is also the advent of satisfaction, that central principle of economics, politics and morality. Taller for a start: the average size of the kings of France, judged by the suits of armour displayed in the Musée de la Guerre at the Invalides and the arrays of once-glorious scrap iron ranged along the galleries of great chateaux, is astonishingly small by our standards; we are giants compared to those midgets. It is stronger too, faster, better maintained. Our athletes make a mockery of their grandparents' feats of strength, skill and endurance. The slowest marathon runner in the French team would beat the Athenian who brought the news of the victory at Marathon by an hour, and without dying of exhaustion. The fact is that the very object of performance has changed. At Nantes in the late 1960s, the poor cross-country skiers running round the Parc de Procé had to listen to their trainer, an Algeria veteran, repeating the motto 'easy training, hard war; hard training, easy war'; war was still the ultimate male experience. Why should it not be the ultimate aspiration too? Athletics trainers used to extol training as a way of transcending pain; today they extol performance as near-ecstasy for the self, participation in the myth for the spectator. Man used to be born to work and suffer, or worse still to vanquish; now he is born, maintained and embellished to enjoy himself. War waged on the self through asceticism, privation, renunciation prepared the ground for another, the real war, in which individual frustrations were released at a single stroke on the battlefield; with the disappearance of all prospect of war on the frontiers (of the nation, of the faith, of the party), war against the self no longer has meaning. More than that: struggle must be waged against all frustrations; the satisfaction of all desires must be organized; pacification comes at that price. The morality of satisfaction is replacing the morality of repression. And the same morality weighs on the experience of labour itself: required to become pleasure, fulfilment, well-being, or failing that a source of guilty conscience.

A detailed history of the transformations of the body visible in its public representations over the past 30 years, for example at work or in war, or in advertising imagery and showplaces—backs straightening, shoulders becoming more assertive, hips moving freely, open hands—would doubtless illustrate how the religion behind the end of religion, Christianity,[7] by instituting the examination of conscience that led people to focus on themselves, and then by permitting and encouraging hedonist representations of the world as a compliment to God, favoured the body's withdrawal from subjection. Rendering to God that which is God's and to Caesar that which is Caesar's was bound to empty heaven of its promises sooner or later; Caesar's share is quite enough for us. Probably too we should learn to see religion in history as the liberation of the body and of desire, through the image of the resurrection of the body, even though dogma still maintains the fiction of repression of the flesh … to put it bluntly, the Christian religion versus the Vatican's word on condoms and divorce.

Loss of the soul

To ensure the good life, to enjoy it in peace, you need to calm the soul and the mind, not to lose your head over nothing. Western philosophy

7. See Marcel Gauchet, *Le désenchantement du monde*, Gallimard, 1985.

and religion had worked in common to put down a body that was the 'profane garment of the soul', an enemy of eternal salvation being capable of desire, capable of pleasure and folly, hence of sin ... a body cut off from heaven and from God, unlike its equivalent elsewhere, in India and China for example. Its most emblematic representation is still the painting by Hieronymus Bosch, of Saint Anthony being assailed by earthly temptations. Now this curse is turned inside out; the body capable of giving and receiving pleasure is capable of goodness in that it gives that very pleasure and gives it again, takes it and takes it again, calls for it and shouts about it. We are close to making pleasure a duty, almost an obligation; the slaves of entertainment, of satisfied leisure, of sporting or amorous performance, on the track, in saunas or clubs, follow without knowing it Talleyrand's maxim—'every day not devoted to pleasure is a day wasted'—to the point of letting it become a new source of pressure, stress even. To consume leisure, seek out one's pleasure, at any cost and in every way, is becoming yet another social constraint whose novelty does nothing to reduce its force: what a joy to do nothing, and what a taboo as well! The space of life is the space of the pleasure of life—of the pleasures of living—and it belongs to me alone. Morality no longer has anything to do with it, except for the morality that forbids the destruction or degradation of this body's life space through abuse. On the contrary: it is the community that is always brought up short, face to face with the limits it aspires less and less to impose on the infinite space of the pleasures of living, now viewed as rights.

The body and the mind, of course, are seeing their relations transformed. Recognition of the primacy of the body places muscles, bones, sexual organs, skin, where soul, mind and intelligence used to be: overhanging everything. The decline of religions, ideologies, world systems, goes further than the questioning of this or that system, religion or ideology; it is the ability to believe, to think, to construct, that we have come to distrust. 'Stop trying to mess with my head' is our world's response to anyone who might aspire to return to examinations of conscience. It is a grave accusation among teenagers. Thinking has to be mistrusted: too much harm has been caused by believing in, thinking about, dreaming of a better world for that sort of thing to be seen as harmless. Those who promised to 'change things' did too much harm to have any credit left. Two European wars that dragged in the rest of the world, the empires of evil that emerged from some of the finest minds Europe ever trained, provide some justification for this revulsion against religious, political and moral functions.

Rematerializing the world

> Another disenchantment is spreading as knowledge of the brain supplies a more material basis for those functions that once seemed to come under the soul. When some brain operations, successful in their own terms, lead to loss of religious faith; when others modify marital or amorous fidelity, or the ability to keep to undertakings, the rematerialization of the world takes a sharp and problematic turn. The question of beliefs, of beauty, of what is good and beneficial, is being reduced to neuropsychological mechanical engineering. And the fiction of immaterial savings bursts like a bubble; savings in future will be material, because they are for the benefit of the body.

Technology plays a powerful role in liberating the body from its old terrors and its apparent subjections; we had already been delivered from the burden of memory by the invention and diffusion of printed books; now we are promised delivery from intelligence, analysis and reasoning by machines that can think. The great struggle with pain that began with the market launch of aspirin (1899 in France) is ending victoriously, if very late; now anxiety, anomie and depression are the targets of new solutions combining cosmetics, pharmacology and psychotropic drugs. The current thrust of the neurobiological sciences challenges morality, to liberate the body from it. It explains some of the most complex human behaviours—religious faith, conjugal fidelity, long-term investment—in terms of pure cerebral mechanics. That is how the areas of the frontal lobes involved in religious fervour were accurately located; after brain operations, certain patients became mystical; others who had possessed faith were dismayed to find they no longer had any religious feeling. Much the same applies to sexual infidelity, the appetite for conquest, sexual delinquency (with some sex offenders the probability of re-offending is 100 per cent; hence the proposals for surgical or chemical castration); purely a matter of cerebral mechanics, or so some neurobiologists claim! And the development of neuroeconomics, which tries to reconcile the science of living matter with economic science, explaining market fluctuations by reference to the cerebral modalities of long- or short-term choice, confirms it, or claims to. It is not in the immaterial but in the body that we must seek and find the laws of behaviour, including the laws obeyed by operators in financial markets.

New, and stupefying, is the revelation that the body is rarer—more difficult to reproduce, extend or deputize for—than the mind. The digital revolution, information technology and artificial intelligence ensure the body's revenge on the soul, the mind and the other foggy entities in which religions, ideologies and mysticisms used to find a foothold. It promises to deliver us from such cumbersome virtues as application, merit and determination, which have done us so much harm. America has yet to learn from Europe that virtues kill just as surely as vices; more so perhaps. Our everyday reality is made largely by virtual, digital slaves who are learning very thoroughly how to dispense with memory, analysis, reason and judgement; so thoroughly that the possibility of attributing criminal responsibility to intelligent systems is currently being mooted; so thoroughly that some are already eyeing immortality via the fabrication of an intelligent avatar, a cyborg, equipped with their memories, their intelligence and preferences. Information technology, by way of its enormous jumps in power and sophistication and its equally enormous downward jumps in cost, has arrived at the unforeseen: the suggestion of mental prostheses, prostheses of memory, skill or knowledge. The machine can substitute itself for the mind; indeed it is already doing so. At the end of a fantastic inversion, the thing that remains most human, irremediably human, is this body capable of suffering, capable of enjoyment, capable of feeling. That primacy of the body can deploy all the more smoothly when the imagination is effectively corralled by television and interactive games, when the attention focused on the world is channelled and diverted by the internet, when the media set the limits on judgement and when systems for producing representation, inquiry and images determine everyone's preferences ... the powers that be, authorities of every sort, can ignore the body all the more easily for the unprecedented grip they are guaranteed on the mind. Time was when schools needed a lot of surveillance to keep occupied for every moment of the day the bodies of children inclined by nature to all sorts of excesses: running, shouting, fighting, chasing each other; from the 7 a.m. bell in the dormitory to lights out at 10 not a minute without supervision, management, discipline. Now it takes nothing more than a games console, cable TV or internet connection to occupy the same children without respite; their digital excesses trouble no one.

Those who spoke of human capital used to divert quickly into immaterial capital: mind, intelligence, creativity, innovation, values. They were wrong. The body is all that remains to us of the real. The paths of the immaterial lead into the swamps of the soul. What centuries were lost there, what myriad lives wasted in the struggle with the self! The augmentation of human capacities no longer lies in a cultural and moral progress that the twentieth century taught us to distrust—what nations were more civilized than Germany and Austria during the early 1900s, even up to 1930?—but in the technical improvement of the body's performances. Biotechnologies, nanotechnologies, the human capital—which will determine the economy of the coming decade—is complete in that body whose mind is its instrument, in its service, and never tires of ransacking the recesses of the intelligence for means to a more complete well-being and short-cuts to help unveil a new pleasure in living.

It is as if the body had emancipated itself from the state, the prevailing order, the group, at the exact moment that it is becoming more dependent for its production and reproduction on demanding and costly public systems. Piercings, voluntary mutilations, the implantation of intelligent microchips under the skin, make it clear: my body is my property. *Usus et* (increasingly) *abusus*, but individual, my doing and not the king's, the general's or the law's. Encouraged by the ideology of human rights and its inconsistencies, the privatization of the body is the first and most important privatization: are there really any others? But interpretations of this shift are very diverse even inside developed states. Some US states still impose penal sanctions for some sexual practices between consenting adults. Every night in Berlin, Paris or London sees a widening of the long-hidden gap that causes fun-loving Westerners and militant humanists to feel that one side of the Atlantic loves weapons and death, while the other loves pleasure and life. To help judge this, try the Bar Bar in rue Championnet, the fetishist nights featuring Demonia and Electra at Sorlut's in rue Lepic, the 2 Plus 2 or the Kit-Kat Club in Berlin. Discussion of investment opportunities in 'vice houses', centred on an Australian brothel, has even penetrated the august columns of the *Wall Street Journal* (in May 2004). At what rate of profit in percentage terms does the source of the dividends pale into insignificance? It seems impulsive to refer the matter to Puritanism or Protestantism … and Berlin and Amsterdam, a long way off after all… More than a nuance separates the two sides of the Atlantic: the break between a society of the project, which continues to treat the frontiers of the world and history as a challenge, and societies that would rather not know where their frontiers are, and see history as a succession of moments to be lived, without risk, without import and without meaning.

Across all these developments and disconnections a new form of truth, a new regime, is bringing about the advent of the body. To mention hedonism and leave it at that means you have perceived nothing of the world that is coming, the world of bodies. For the old-time Christian, for today's Muslim fundamentalist, the world of the faith, its apostles and saints, its rituals and intercessions, was more real than the world beneath his feet, the world surrounding him, but perceived only faintly, foggily, through the convolutions of belief. To the upright citizen of today, man or woman, the real is that which speaks to the body as sensation, as experience, as enjoyment or as representation. The advent of the body is fabricating a new reality, one that serves the body, comforts it and reaches out to it; and the world that is coming will be illegible, unworkable, to anyone outside the kingdom of the body, of its satisfaction, its desire, its well-being. A new regime of truth is under construction. The good, the true and the beautiful are being recomposed; a new reality is in labour.

A changed ending

> Happiness counteracts old age.
>
> Franz Kafka

> Nothing confirms and proves the sovereign being of God and His dominion over us better than the fact of death.
>
> Bossuet, Sermon on Death to the Daughters of the Visitation of Our Lady

Long life, money and abundance, peace, the production of life, change the body in every aspect. Even death, death above all, is changed. Is it because the gods have fled that death, for the first time, can be looked in the face? Or is it because the growl of war cannot be heard from any direction? Because we die in hospital beds or the retirement home instead of on the battlefield or down the mines or in the fields? Some, indeed many, intend to choose their death as they were able to choose their lives. Some, indeed many, have listened to their parents—paralysed, afflicted with Parkinson's or cancer—speaking of death as a promise and a hope for too long, and too often, not to understand what they meant. The history of bodies, the history of the subject and his word, the history of the naked and the dead, is rushing into the unknown. The discovery of long life and its scrambling of all frontiers encourages us to expect the transformation now taking place, a transformation in which everything—almost everything—of the game of life and death is at stake, or has been, or will be.

It means the end of the body, of course. This body is new in that the old curse of death has withdrawn to the fringes, the sidelines. Death always used to be an accident. The painter Géricault died at 30 in a fall from a horse, and an heir to the French throne, the comte de Provence adored by the French and mourned by Châteaubriand, in a runaway coach; Prince Napoleon, exiled among British colonial troops, was killed by a Zulu assegai at 26; Spanish influenza or cholera carried off Casimir Périer. A few years ago, I nearly had to have a finger amputated after getting a rose thorn under the nail—60 years earlier I might have died from general infection with tetanus, gangrene or something of the sort. Nothing unusual about it: I knew a Nantes gardener, mad on roses, who died of tetanus at 56. That was in 1960, in rue de la Ville-aux-Roses. And I knew the grandchildren of a former soldier of poor Marshal Bazaine, who on the way back from the campaign against the Prussians in 1870 tried to kill a rabid wolf that was devastating local flocks, was bitten by it, and ended up suffocated between two mattresses by his fellows on the grounds that the rabies made him a danger to others. That was in rue de Derrière-la-Muraille, Saint-Jean du Bruel, in the Aveyron. Some of the grandchildren of conscripts in the same intake were still telling the tale, without thinking it out of the ordinary. Nothing unusual about it: death was just there. The whole of life was marked by suffering and death, permanent companions of believing, ageing and living; slumped back, bowed shoulders, curved spine; suffering almost a daily experience; death by infection, epidemic, poisoning, agricultural or industrial accident, a real prospect at every moment. But what does that matter when life is a mere rite of passage, a dry run for eternity? Religion gives these things a mystical meaning; it goes further, teaching that suffering and death provide what meaning life has; visible in the mirror all along the road, suffering and death are the essential object of whatever man can know or discover by himself; knowledge and learning are concentrated on this path from which we can see no obvious way out; or are there many ways out? The *Ars moriendi* is a literary exercise present everywhere, although Dances of Death, those baroque funereal frenzies, are abolished from public space and survive only through oblivion. When a preacher, a Bossuet or Fénelon among many others, wished to establish his authority and summon people to confession or penitence, all he had to do was thunder from his pulpit: 'You, at whom my finger is pointing: perhaps God's finger is pointing at you too, perhaps you will die tomorrow.' Time was the dimension inseparable from the body, and the actual chance of death the counterpoint to each day. Who could resist the oft-emphasized meaning and the lure of eternity to cross that wall? In gaining long life, we have lost eternity. Or rather, because we have lost eternity and its renunciations, we have wrested long life from the gods, from sickness, from death. And that conquest is only the beginning.

A life without suffering

The body and suffering, still. This Western body is new in its ability to pass through an entire lifetime without ever suffering, really suffering. The historical backwardness of France in treating pain, in eliminating the shameful abandonment of sick or post-operative patients to their suffering, is being rapidly made up. The struggle against pain has become a recognized public health imperative, until it is succeeded by priority given to the patient's well-being, and until perhaps assistance to chosen death becomes a necessary further priority in the interests of human dignity. From the morphine patch through the whole range of analgesics and tranquillizers, pain management is at a point where some people, suffering from incurable illnesses, will reach the end of the road without having really suffered—give or take that loss of focus, that gentle fog that carries both the outside world and the self off into the distance, along with the pain. This body is new in that it goes through life without suffering any more, or any differently, than it has chosen to suffer: serious devotees of sports or extreme sports, adepts of long hikes in mountains or wilderness, are seeking confusedly to renew in the experience of pain, the laboured breath or muscles begging for respite, the threads of a relation that is being lost and a memory that is escaping ... what can we read, see, understand of all those whose cry was primarily a cry of suffering, a cry against suffering and the death it announced? What can we understand of Pascal who lived all his life, from the age of 20, in a tunic of pain? What can we share with them of what was called, for so long, the human condition, which used to mean intimate acquaintance with suffering from birth and permanent companionship with death?

So is death without suffering—soon to be relieved of fear too and perhaps of moral scruples—going to enter the universe of choice and will? Some countries are already reviving what was once the honour of dying by one's own hand, the loftiest of choices. The law that allows a fully aware sick person in Holland or Belgium to obtain (after several requests) medical help in ending his or her life with dignity, and the marketing in Belgium of a pharmaceutical suicide kit, suggest a new relationship with a body that no longer has to suffer to live, or to die. Prepared, somewhat timidly, by the public debate over the 'Humbert affair' (the trial of a mother for helping her incurably disabled child to die), the French law on the right to 'allow to die' adopted on 13 April 2005 brought nothing new on the matter of death with dignity, but helped to break down the wall of silence surrounding the 150,000 to 200,000 annual decisions to 'unplug' terminally ill patients from their life support equipment: decisions taken outside any juridical framework, decisions left to nurses, sometimes taken under pressure to free up beds for new admissions. Awareness of death and the inevitable confrontation with pain made humanity what it is and drove it onward and upward; the very earliest human traces are funerary paintings and ornaments; art and the gods were born from the chance of suffering and death, the delirium of illness. To be better, the body had to be ignored, or vanquished. How many, over the millennia, have played out their passing eternities giving their whole lives to it? Stylites, hermits, anchorites, sanyassins ... a cohort of desperate insects battering themselves senseless against the impenetrable window of the body!

That dream has deserted us. To live well now a person has to become aware of his body, inhabit his body, get inside his body. What can we understand of religions and mysticisms without knowing that daily brotherhood with suffering? The knight Ignatius of Loyola endured without a word the long torture of a badly-knit fracture that had to be rebroken and reset, before taking the road north that would lead him to found the Society of Jesus—the Jesuit order—on the steps of Montmartre; the procession of the ill-clad, the lame, the hunchbacked, the crippled, those mutilated in glory or infamy who were Marshals of France, popes, great lords, bemedalled heroes tortured by gout, what can we understand of them? Priests talked to them about their souls. It would not have taken a lot of words to make them believe in a better world than this vale of tears. We today have a number of reasons for doubting that it exists, starting with the excellence of this one, an Eden of abundance, a Disneyworld of permanent entertainment. They used to promise to free man of his bodily destiny; we want to live it out to the end, that destiny of pleasure, well-being and experiences. And anything that takes away any part of this body's aptitude for experience, for attraction, for pleasure, is a theft: as intolerable as the theft of fire is the theft of life.

Life and the choice of life, and finally the choice of death. A seminar was held in Paris on 13 November 2007 by the Judaeo-Christian Friendship Association under the title 'From the fear of sudden death to a diminished life'.[8] In other words, the fear of dying, of a slow abandonment of the self, of old age, has replaced the fear of death itself. Suicide has not been a crime since 1791. But it remained a failure, a defect, a scandal. For the first time, men and women faced with long life, with becoming tired of their existence in a world slipping away from them, are demanding a last freedom, to end life when they want to or in conditions they have defined in advance, before the onset of impotence, senility or final decline. For the first time, a person's body is what the person chooses to make of it—to an ever-increasing extent, and for an ever-increasing number of humans. For the first time, reproducing yourself, suffering, ageing, dying are escaping from nature's dominion, or giving us reason to dream of that fine leap forward. Lifespan will not escape management and choice. It is entering the domain of the will: by 2004 the association Dignitas—which under Professor Ludwig Minelli runs an 'assisted suicide clinic' in Zurich, Switzerland, the only one in the world—had 3,000 names from all over Europe on its waiting lists. We wanted freedom for bodies, now we have become responsible for that freedom, thus dependent. We are subject to a new duty of management, unforeseen, worrying, tyrannical: the duty of managing our lifespan and the production of our lifespan ... and even perhaps controlling the time of death.

How will we contrive to manage what no one until now has ever had the terrifying privilege of managing: deciding on life and death without being in the heat of love, battle, hatred or passion? And how do we make ourselves choose what no one before us has ever needed to choose? In the anxiety over the future that afflicts Europeans, this question—the excessive responsibility that an unprecedented control over life forces them to assume, and the power over the self that it confers—counts for more than is generally recognized.

---

8. The lecture is available at www.amitie-judeo-chretienne.fr.

The body is changing death

> Faith, like a jackal, feeds among the tombs, and even from these dead doubts she gathers her most vital hope.
>
> Herman Melville, *Moby Dick*

> The Tchouktches, a small tribe of Siberian fishermen and herders living in the frozen North-East opposite Alaska, seem to be almost alone in having developed a culture of voluntary and socialized death: the elderly, when left alone and unable to work, their children raised, could choose to depart from this life by asking a friend or neighbour to stab or strangle them, voluntary death being celebrated as a valorous act preferable to sinking into old age. In its gentle and kindly humanity, the Soviet Union set out to liberate the Tchouktches from what the Russian officials sent to govern their territories saw as criminal behaviour. The effort succeeded, thanks to Soviet police efficiency and the liberal distribution of vodka to a population wholly unfamiliar with strong spirits. There is no voluntary death in the Tchouktche lands now, because there are no Tchouktches left. The recent appointment of the Russian plutocrat Roman Abramovich—a London resident and owner of Chelsea football club—as governor of Tchouktchekia seems unlikely to bring them back to life.

Following the suicide of Roger Quilliot, mayor of Clermont-Ferrand and Minister of Housing during François Mitterrand's presidency, Gabrielle Wittkop ended her life in December 2002. Quilliot had found it unbearable to have to leave office owing to age and reduced mobility, Gabrielle Wittkop did not want to live through the terminal stages of lung cancer. Both loved life, and their friends and families, and had lived to the full. Wittkop had earlier told *Libération*, on 4 January 2001: 'Death is the most important moment in life. On my birthday, my friends wish me good health and hope my work is going well, but no one ever thinks of saying "I wish you a good death, Gabrielle"...'.[9]

Life ... no one gets out of it alive. That at least (but for how long?) is still unchanged. The ultimate question for this transformed body concerns the end of life. And it faces us with a frontier, a frontier that some approach with a firm tread: the frontier of chosen death. Whether through passive or active euthanasia, or through the voluntary act of ending an isolated, painful or purposeless life, even through being allowed to die when the will to live has gone, the scale of the phenomenon is not caused solely by

9. Quoted by Mathieu Lindon, *Libération*, 24 December 2002.

the lengthening of lifespan but also by the isolation that results from it. It underlines the novelty of a relation to death that is above all, in a different way, a relation to the body, to the vision of a body for living in, to the vision of a life that is more social and emotional than biological. What is left to die of a body from which all life—all pleasure, all projects, all relationships—has withdrawn?

'We will all die through euthanasia', headlined a Belgian daily paper in January 2008. The article traced a development already broadly under way in northern Europe. Belgium and Holland adopted laws on euthanasia in 2001 and 2002. Switzerland practises it in implicit fashion. In these countries, according to a 2006 study conducted by 'European end of life decision', a third of deaths are sudden; a quarter to a half follow decisions that may hasten death, most often painkilling drugs (24 per cent in Italy, 50 per cent in Switzerland), followed by withdrawal or cessation of treatment (21 per cent in Switzerland), and lastly assisted or unassisted voluntary death in 0.7 per cent to 3 per cent of cases.[10]

Once a family production as rendered by Greuze in all its emotional fervour and dramatic tension, an individual act, for many the most personal and sometimes the most remarkable in a life devoted to modest achievements and willing obedience, death has been gradually stolen from life and from the living by the medical system with the help of psychotropic drugs. Little by little, death has stopped being, even for those who have the chance, an act, a proof of the self, and lapsed into a sort of prescribed unconsciousness, a relentless, invisible, socially costly and individually unpleasant decline. Our societies do not stint on the means required for the medical machinery to suppress awareness of death in the dying person, of the approach of death in their family or friends, and suffering in both cases, conjuring both death and the deceased out of sight in an opaque process of socialization. Given this de facto state of things—caused in part by the generalization of death in hospital and the concentration of 80 per cent of sickness insurance on the last six months of French lives, but also by the prolongation of life in aged individuals who are hemiplegic for example—the long or very long lifespan is starting to undermine a consensus that has never been debated in the public arena. The cruelty of prolonging the lives of gravely handicapped people with no hope of remission is explained by a collective shirking of responsibility,

10. See the January 2007 issue of the INED journal *Population et société*.

by cowardice. A decision may have to be taken to put an end to abusive treatment; but none is needed to continue it. Helping someone to die may mean assuming responsibility; keeping them alive does not. A country doctor, with the tools he had, starting with his own awareness, used to do the refereeing himself; he decided when to withdraw care or end treatment. These days, the first concern of a hospital doctor when a death occurs is to justify himself: we did all we should have done right to the end. This does not mean 'we responded to the patient's requirement', or 'we satisfied the expectations of the nearest and dearest'. It means 'no one can say a word against us'.

Protecting the dignity of the human individual means allowing him to make his death the final act of a life lived in freedom. More and more people, anonymous or celebrated, want the ending of their lives be an act, a voluntary acquiescence and a choice, medically assisted or not. From those old people with cancer who refuse chemotherapy to ancients who reject the *n*th operation for stiff joints or yet another update on a prosthesis that no longer works properly, manifestations of this acquiescence in departure, this demand that the ending of life be a last act of freedom and responsibility, are becoming more frequent with the lengthening of lifespan. The case of the three brothers all diagnosed with cancer between the ages of 61 and 65 each of whom, without discussing it with the others, chose to reject all treatment, looks like a new model of behaviour in confronting the end of life, and its reconquest. It is a little as if, at the very end of this long, very long life that we have given ourselves, the body wearing out counted for less than the withdrawal of the world, and vertigo before the big sleep. And a little as if, faced with this relinquishment surreptitiously organized by the medical and hospital system, those reaching the end of their long, very long lives wished to reclaim themselves until the last possible moment, and assert to the very end their capacity to act and to be.

Choice of ending

Does the self-programming by man of the evolution of his species and of his own lifespan constitute an insult to God, who is the loser? This new situation common to all the developed countries, the fruit of technical advances achieved in the last two decades of the twentieth century, is being further boosted by the development of nanotechnologies during the first years of the twenty-first. The question that dominated geriatrics 10 or 20 years ago was the biological ceiling of life expectancy, with the consequence that operations were not carried out on the over-eighties; certain observations posited an irremediable ageing between 90 and 110, when only very intensive medication could make possible serious surgical operations, for example. It was commonly accepted that the rapid increase in life expectancy would slow, then stop, as all the major elements—end of pandemics, advances in hygiene and nutrition, spread of good practices in physical exercise, putting smoking, drinking and dangerous driving on the social index, generalization of basic medical services—had their full effects.

This rational attitude is no more. Treated after fracturing the neck of a femur, a great-grandmother of 99 can reach her century on her feet and functioning. After an operation to remove a tumour, a nonagenarian chain-smoker feels that the illness has gone. Those limited prospects are succeeded by an unlocatable horizon of life promised to new bodies that are increasingly—for new parts, for vital systems, for more and more organs—products of the biological industry. Nothing is left in theory to prevent the demolition of ceilings generally considered impassable. Nothing biological at least; culture, the clock of one's self-awareness in society, for one's family, is becoming the principal cause of mortality in men and women not so much really worn out as obsolete; the indicator of self-satisfaction leading them to choose death in preference to an ever-growing private awareness of their uselessness. To choose, and no longer to undergo, since neither nature nor ageing are enough by themselves to interrupt a biological existence capable of being prolonged indefinitely, but that has become socially and individually meaningless.

Will the conquest of death as choice and act of will be the major arrival of this decade? It would mark a decisive step away from the empire of the religious, emancipation from ancient terrors, an escape from God's dominion over us. The demand that death be a final voluntary, conscious and above all chosen act is the outcome of the demand for life as private property, as the ultimate domain for the exercise of individual choice, the deployment of individual will and the assertion of individual dignity. It is no coincidence that many of those who have chosen their deaths in a thoughtful and voluntary manner are people who have participated in public life and exercised political responsibility. Perhaps it is here that the choice to be an actor in life finds its fulfilment, its last frontier and its transcendence.

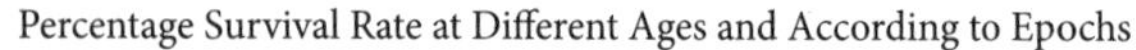
Percentage Survival Rate at Different Ages and According to Epochs

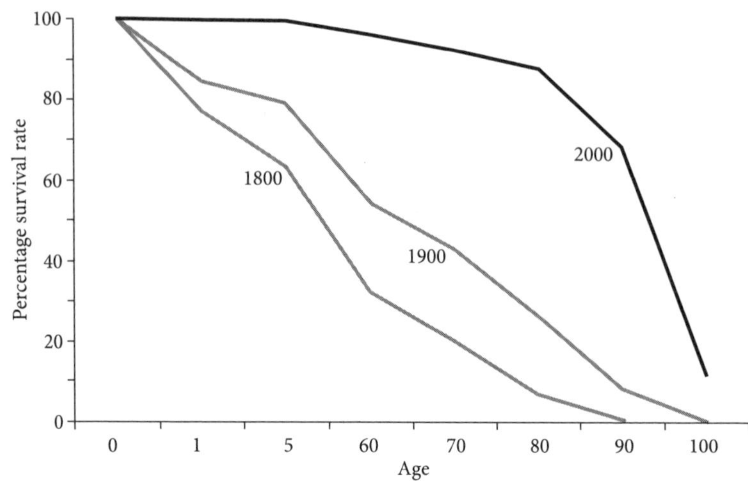

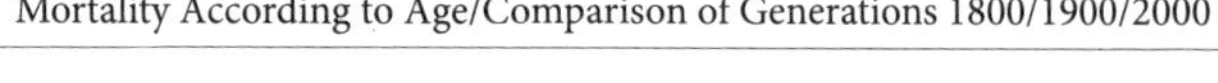
Mortality According to Age/Comparison of Generations 1800/1900/2000

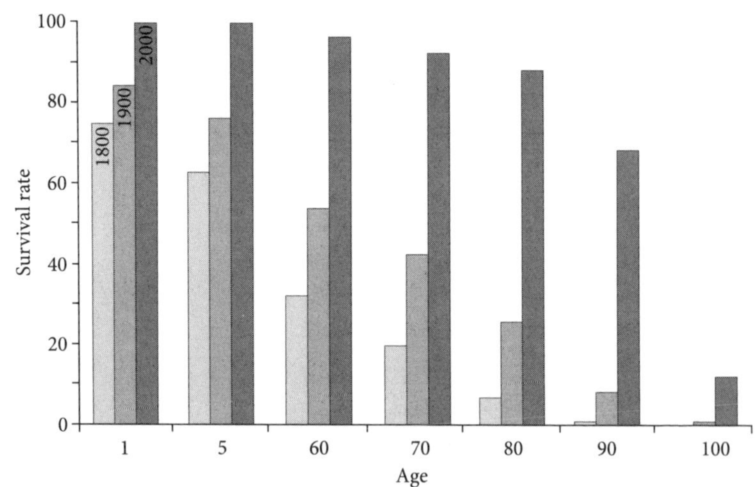

A new familiarity, still hesitant, is taking shape. Books which offer to help people to die well start by explaining the need for their readers to sign their name on the flyleaf; to domesticate the idea of the end, to appropriate the end of life. Personal testimonies encourage men and women who want to choose the day and time for themselves to accompany others in their terminal phase. The ending of religious interdicts bearing on suicide, on the voluntary transformation of the body, liberates personal choices in an area that used to be closed to them. Movements for dignity at the end of life ask a question: are we capable of moving on to the chosen life ending? After the privatization of the body and the life space, are we really going to privatize the ending of life and make it our business? Who will be first to demand their own death, to appropriate that unique and ultimate experience of life, and take away from the hospital and the anti-depressants their function of removal of the self?

The collective question raised by this other great transformation addresses the religions, and it is a harsh one. The religions of the Book have done very well out of the fear of death: like Bossuet, thundering warnings from his pulpit to beautiful princesses and elegant dukes that God could reclaim the gift of life at any moment. That is all over. Fear of death no longer feeds religious sentiment. From this standpoint—which a war or major catastrophe could obviously transform—what would religion have to say on how to live and die, except by playing the role of moral authority to which part of the French episcopate has reverted? Still from this standpoint, if religions want to be something other than the rapacious, corpse-guzzling birds of ill omen denounced by Melville, how are they to go about becoming religions of life, of living-plus? Let the men of faith learn to talk about religions as religions of good living, in the sense used by Michel Foucault in *L'archéologie du savoir*; surely that is a condition that would make them audible again, speaking a language audible to those who, delivered from fear of death and freed from other fears, are still not living as well as all that. The supposed developments in the critical areas of sexual morality, birth and formal or informal marriage seem to answer the new anthropology required by the conditions of conception, ego formation, autonomy, relations with others and the ending of life, without really seeming insurmountable compared to the historical journey completed by the religious verities so far. After all, the Catholic church forbade lending money at interest for six centuries.

The conquest of death as something acted out, chosen, voluntary, is the final stage of the invention of a new body. And it cannot fail to inflect social forms in general, death having weighed so heavily on collective institutions in the past through the agency of war, accident, murder or execution. Rather than acceptance of medically assisted death or even euthanasia, what has to be found here is a new area of law and a new dimension of responsibility. One that involves an unexpected bypassing of religion, a wasting away of eternity, of salvation and the pitfalls of the soul, in the hope of achieving the serene reconciliation of life with time, with age, and with its own end. The advent of the body is also this disappearance of death into choice and will; an advent that uproots the religions from the soil of fear in which they once thrived. Death should be imagined as the last act of those who have chosen to put an end to a life so long, so full and so fulfilled that any extension in years, weeks or even minutes could only detract from satisfaction with the self. An honourable life should be imagined as resembling that of the Hindus who when the chosen moment comes take a room in a 'Stay and die' hotel in Benares, close to the ghats where their ashes will be scattered beneath the drifting smoke, the endless circling of vultures … ready to sign off a story that has gone on long enough, by choice, in dignity and in hope.

2. Production of the Body

The end of the land dates from yesterday. Its suddenness took us by surprise, caused the gods to fall silent and the blood to pulse less vigorously in our temples. And the loss of the land has seized us with vertigo, we who remain its products, along with our images, our language, our representations. Only derision can mask our distress over the vast departure of what made us what we are—French, European, from this land or that—when our wealth was still under our feet.

Now that our wealth is in our heads, we must play at being what we no longer are; the mere spectacle of nature is expected to disarm our vertigo over the loss of origins. With the loss of the land, what we ought to be talking about is the end of duty as it has shaped us over the millennia: taking a husband or wife, nurturing one's own, preparing for the next season, keeping house, putting something aside for a rainy day will never have the same meaning again. With the loss of the land, what we ought to be talking about is the loss of wealth as it has shaped us; owning, inheriting, will never have the same meaning again.

The effects of this loss of the land are everywhere. They are making mutants of us. For the land, its harvests, its silences, its images and words took thousands of years to produce—with stooped back, hollow chest, short breath and knock knees—those now aspiring to free themselves of it, and in under a century, just two or three generations. For the land which used to define distance, the frontier, duration, the bond; the land which used to produce certainty of oneself and others, remains a producer of reality in the words, images, representations and social structures that it still haunts, and that are reproduced out of habit. Despite quantum and relativity theories, which have located their limits and exposed the illusions in their meanings, the laws of nature, terrestrial attraction, gravitation, mass, continue to explain our sensations and still underlie our representations. In our sayings, place-names, verbal short cuts, habits of thought, we remain mentally the heirs of what shaped our parents and forebears. In less than two centuries, European populations, 90 per cent of which used to live by working the land and exploiting animal and human strength, have been attracted or compelled to go to work in factories, offices and a wide variety of service jobs. In the 50 years between 1946 and 1996 the French agricultural population lost 5,300,000 workers, the population of farmers and farm workers dropping from six million to 700,000. That represents an average fall of more than 100,000 a year, 're-structuring' on a scale experienced by no other economic sector. The break with the land as nature, reality and truth has been achieved in the European Union: the land used to give us the world through our senses, through muscles and the body; now a new alliance of the body and the virtual is giving us the world on screen, through signs and representations.

We should take note of the virtual disappearance on this side of the Atlantic of work based solely on animal or human physical strength, while Canada and the US continue to pay tribute to physical labour in the figures of the lumberjack, long-distance trucker and Texan cowboy. The French and European law that forbids the handling of any weight over 20 kilograms without some form of mechanical assistance is ensuring that; meanwhile representation of the American worker remains focused on the action, the grasp, the materiality of the movement. A Roman Gaul from the palatial villa country of the Rhône valley, a Mediterranean olive or vineyard cultivator, a Calabrian blacksmith, would have found easy understanding with a French peasant or artisan of the 1940s. Men of sinew and muscle, of sweat and straining effort. All of those, hardly separable from each other over two millennia, receded from us steadily over the last 50 years of the twentieth century. And there are so many still, men of the French earth, living like internal immigrants in a country that no longer speaks their language, no longer shares their values, no longer *understands* them!

There are considerable consequences. Physical consequences, on stature, musculature, nutrition … and defects too: bad backs are an invention of the tertiary sector—office work—and some doctors are predicting an unprecedented increase in psychomotor and skeleto-muscular problems owing to the disappearance from work of any physical dimension. Not all fatigue is bad! Consequences in the relation with life, sex and birth, that companionship with animals connected with a nature, once commonplace and obvious, that has become an obsession with us. Consequences for the family, which the land had organized over thousands of years to ensure its cultivation, pass on its ownership, give birth to those who would fertilize it; the earth that gives life, the earth that clothes the bodies from which life has departed. What does a person know of life who has not seen a tree grow? Consequences for married life, when child and old person both need full support. In a world of paid workers, where it is the job not the work that earns the income, housekeeping by women means losing a salary. Salaried work makes possible the 'dinky' ('double income, no kids') development being tried in Europe and imitated worldwide. Social consequences for life plans, when the nature of the salary and work contract becomes the key to the new world of credit, the immediate spending of future income (or in other words, agreed future subjection to the labour market system, in exchange for a better life now).

The essential transformation is not between farm work and factory work but between selling the product of one's labour and selling one's labour, thus entering waged society. Between self and self, business and the market have established themselves. Populations which used to draw their resources from their own products, either directly by consuming them or indirectly by selling them, now drew their resources from the sale of their labour to an enterprise for a salary; the subsequent individualization of wages or salaries transformed family relations. It turned children and the elderly into net costs on the family where formerly they had been a resource, contributing to the family's output to the extent of their means: whether on the land, in the forge or around the workshop, no child is too small or grandmother too ancient to do something useful. The North African and Chinese businesses in French city centres—increasingly deserted by traditional retailers—are a living illustration, mobilizing as they do three or four generations in the service of one priority: giving the customer what he wants.

This technical revolution, promoted under the banner of progress and constant augmentation of capacities to produce and act, has strained the relation with nature, but without putting anything in its place. The world has become an available object. This has liberated Western man, to a very large extent, from want, danger, and the violence of the elements. It has relieved him of the soil, of subjection to its rhythms, its timelessness, its weight. It has given Europeans a mastery over their environment, far and near, never before attained or even dreamed of. Here again, Europe is drifting apart from the North American continent which—from Montreal blizzards to annual Florida hurricanes—continues to live at the mercy of a hostile environment that has to be faced down. Heroic representations of firemen, truckers and lumberjacks as seen in *USA Today* or TV broadcasts from Fox News or CNBC, or in stories by Jim Harrison, are continuous reminders of the close and impassioned bond still maintained with nature, alternately dominant and dominated, strongly sexualized in the ways it is grasped and confronted, and projected as that which labour possesses and fertilizes (the family likeness between representations of labour in the US and the propaganda films made in Stalinist Russia is striking, in the material confrontation being staged between the human body and the elements, forest, fields, blizzards, etc. How long must we wait for a history of bodies through films: *The Grapes of Wrath* to *Manhattan*, *Modern Times* to *Pulp Fiction*, *Paths of Glory* to *Saving Private Ryan*?)

In Europe, the work of leaving nature has been completed. Trucker and farm labourer do nothing to pump up their muscles: they pilot large machines through power-assisted controls in air-conditioned cabins, in touch by radio, listening to music on the stereo. Winter and summer go by without the fruit or vegetables on the table, the ambient temperature in the house, the available light for working or reading, reminding anyone of the season. Nature and the unchained elements are not frightening any more; progress and technology are what have to be faced down now, because they are frightening the very people to whom they have given so much. A person can live an entire life without really knowing what physical exhaustion is, beyond tiredness, through confrontation with weight, distance, cold or heat, thirst or hunger, and the unravelling of physical and mental forces that it brings. Those fundamental categories of human experience, of the senses and emotions, that distance, weight and duration used to be have been turned upside down. Filipinos and Indonesians experienced September 11 live, just as if they were there. Africans and Asians claim to have acquired Jennifer Aniston or Brad Pitt as their best friend and role model, via a satellite network. Adolescents receive far more incitement, excitement and information from their games consoles, iPods or screens—TV, telephone, internet, computer—than from anything at all in the real world, parents and best friends included. The association of internet, mobile phone and credit card marks a rapid leap forward in extracting man from his environment and separating him from all natural determinants (distance, separation, delay, scarcity); from being the product of nature, he is becoming one who chooses and determines it. He was nature's product; now, in a confusing and murky inversion, nature is becoming his product. And because this new world of domination—imperialism, why not?—advances swathed in the colours of freedom, satisfaction and protection, it is being accepted generally without debate, without guilt, without scrutiny.

With victory over the environment complete, it remains to be achieved over genetics and biology: over the body. That is our present challenge. Meeting it will mean removing the body from the category of nature and making it a product of human activity; man is to become his own finest product. Cloned sheep, test-tube babies, organ banks and gene therapies, supplementary health foods and intelligent prostheses ... the revolution is already under way. Some of its consequences can be glimpsed, usually in the course of argument about some scientific experiment.

Outlets fleetingly open, quickly superseded and replaced by others, into a new world of bodies. A return to cobbled-up certainties about life, death, destiny, human nature ... cobbled, because the heaven of the gods and ideologies remains so dishearteningly empty, because no truth-bearing Word purports these days to reveal the true hidden meaning of things, of the dead and of life. Some of the elements of our historical condition have shifted, so that the experiences of the mystics, scientists, thinkers and sages who since time immemorial have most closely approached the secret of the common condition of humanity have drifted off into a sort of timeless weightlessness, because they are absent from our own historical experience. With every passing day, whether we want to or not, whether we know it or not, we are inaugurating a new human condition. Without knowing it, without wanting it, every woman who takes the pill, every couple awaiting the results of an amniocentesis, every man concealing his Viagra prescription, every regular traveller adjusting his body clock against jetlag with neuromotor stimulants, has crossed the threshold into this new world, without knowing what they are getting into; who does know, after all?

Abandoned as a project by worn-out political ideology, transformation of the human condition is becoming the objective of an improbable partnership between science and the market. Sterility, ageing, menopause, impotence, psychic discomfort, strong emotion, are curable if the market says so and if the cost can be met. This revolution is going to give birth to a new economy, an economy whose raison d'être, whose object and production unit, is the body. Man is to become his own finest product. He will determine himself as a whole, from top to bottom, by himself and for himself. That is what we wanted. Without a plan and without a vision, that is our choice.

Seeking the indeterminate

> When Miss China 2005 made her world tour, her image was striking not so much for its undeniable beauty as for its mutant character. Signs indicative of origin, giving distinctiveness and signalling a membership, are missing from that regular face, its lacquered smile, its programmed gaze. The eyelids have been lifted, the forms slimmed and outline lengthened by liposuction, the skin smoothed and its wrinkles filled by Botox injections, its tone lightened by special creams. Making Miss China one of the early Elect of indeterminacy, programmed to be the Miss of a nowhere world, the fantasized Chosen One of a democratic planet.

The society of invention of the body is a society of indeterminacy. The erasure of the original distinction between sacred and profane, through the slow erasure of the sacred by urban living, calls for the erasure of those distinctions that used to be called age, sex, race, nationality, in a profound and durable overturning of the way of being the self.[1]

Indeterminacy of age, race and nationality. Indeterminacy of gender, species and character. A society is being recomposed from its foundations. And constituting itself on an organized purge of all that binds, that endures, that attaches.

Unlike its predecessors, this society does not fly the banner of the struggle for survival, of the aspiration to go beyond this life for or through a God, but of the dismissal of chance and necessity, those twin species of determination. Peace, wealth, and above all the space of a long lifespan, all encourage this disconnection. It might call itself the economy of liberty, if that word is allowed to keep its ambiguity. No doubt it does liberate, but from what? From the so-called laws of nature, gravitation, mass, which confirmed the quiet evidence of our senses, and which we have already learned to doubt from relativity theory, psychoanalysis and the masters of suspicion. From all the determinisms that limit individual choice, whether of age, gender or belief. Identity is constructed, and it seems to be constructed all the better for the repudiation of what is passed on to it.

---

1. See on this subject Calvin Schrag, *The Self after Postmodernity*, Yale University Press, 1997, which criticizes interestingly the separation of the scientific, ethical, artistic and religious dimensions of life, considered to be characteristic of modernity.

Once provenance is forgotten, all that matters is appearance. The order of representation replaces that of membership, of belonging. With ageing pensioned off, everyone has the age they want and can afford, the age of their choice. With origin erased, crossbreeding offers a vast range of possibilities for tinkering with the self and playing with temporary identities. Its emblematic figure might be David Bowie, an enigmatic adolescent in his sixties, whose unwrinkled face and blond locks render him not so much androgynous as sexless; or Prince, or Iggy Pop subjecting his body to every exercise in ambiguity; or the late Michael Jackson, exemplar of a mutant species of no identifiable race, sex or age. It is no accident that so many of these recent myths are neither men nor women, but blank pages on which anyone can project their fantasies or dreams of belonging, as they do onto the heroes and heroines of their favourite video games. Gay culture, responsible for so many trends in male fashion, is being succeeded by a culture of transsexuality, which combines with crossbreeding to scramble frontiers and thrust back the limits of choice. In the same way, transgressive sexuality is being succeeded by indeterminacy of gender. American universities are doing research that tends to demonstrate the accidental or artificial nature of the sexualization of children; artists (like Orlan or Genesis P-Orridge) are making their bisexed bodies into art works, while Laetitia Casta turned herself into a blond young man with an angel's superhuman gaze, seen through Jean-Paul Goude's lens and filters, achieving the ideal of a human being liberated from origin, gender and belonging, of every determination except the photographer's magic lens at the moment of the shot. When one of New York's most powerful investment banks announces (in February 2008) that in future it will pay for sex-change operations requested by members of its staff, liberation from our origins crosses a new frontier and gives unexpected confirmation to Simone de Beauvoir's famous assertion in *The Second Sex*: 'A woman is not born, but made.' A liberation, no doubt of it; but from what?

The myth of a body without origin, character, country or determination is a powerful presence in fashion, the economy and political discourse. It has given birth to a standard, universal pattern for the bodies of top models; the valued body is born of no one, has come from nowhere, belongs only to its own image, its own will and the market, and is spared from owing anything to anyone. Owing nothing to anyone else; becoming one's own product; juggling with appearances to evade all identifiable descent. 'Orphaned at birth, alone, without family, without patronage, he entered the service at the age of fifteen. He rose through the ranks on merit and each promotion was the fruit of a brilliant action; only the title of Marshal of France could have further embellished, not his own glory, but his example to those who would take him as their model'... The epitaph of François Chevert, lieutenant general of the armies of King Louis XV, a sample of the French language at its best, could be taken as the ideal of a society dreaming of detaching itself from itself. But François Chevert was in the service of his king; we serve ourselves. And if we believe what popular wisdom has to say, a man who is his own master has a pretty poor master. Does 'bettering yourself' still mean anything? What example does it set, and to whom?

And this stage of liberation, detachment or denial is infinitely more violent and basic than any other, since it aims to liberate the individual from determination by blood, genes, gender, age or character as conditions of perceptible experience; to create mutants, escaping from the condition of beings conceived in relations between a man and a woman, born in pain, anxiety and want, and subjected to the hazards of life, doomed to worry and inheriting in an aura of mystery, through the alchemy of heredity, the characteristics of their forebears.

'Reality is what is impossible', Jacques Lacan said. And the body is too real to be tolerated any longer. No cost would be too great if it enabled us to domesticate, to capture, to bear that reality. Just as, over two centuries of rapid and relentless mechanical progress, it came about that things like street lighting, the ambient temperature in dwellings in all weathers, and the presence of snow near ski resorts depend only on the choice of modern humanity, or its preferences and what it is willing to spend, so it is now thought feasible to suspend the random fate of illness or disability on the one hand, and of beauty, attractiveness or physical prowess on the other. Gas lighting, running water on every floor, and penicillin are all parts of the same liberation, or the same exemption from the perceptible universe. Belonging, identity, gender, background, are ruthlessly dismissed from the horizons of the free man in the free market. The substitution of product for reality, as reality, completes the substitution of nature as a product and representation for the nature hailed by Ricardo, 'inexhaustible, indestructible, unalterable in principle'.

Fleeing from the specific

The quest for indeterminacy is pursued with particular vigour in the domain of physical characteristics indicating a membership or betraying an origin. The exemplarity of the transsexuals featured in discussion and reality TV programmes designates a fundamental trend: the rejection of gender. Everyone can choose whether to be a man or a woman; it is not a thing to be decided by an accident of birth. The frenzied hatred of discrimination, for whatever cause or to whatever effect, justifies the return of censorship, reinvents 'thought-crime', and in France sacrifices freedom of expression to moral comfort ... 'there's nothing to it, and anyway it's a bit of a minefield'. This drift, steady for 20 years now, provides another illustration of the withdrawal from nature and of an even more risky attempt to break with reality. Refusing to let age, gender or race have any bearing on the individual's professional, interpersonal, amorous, sporting or artistic capacities has become an article of the collective religion; it is a refusal generally displayed by businesses, directors of Human Resources and head-hunters in the Western world. Here or there it finds anecdotal or climactic expressions, for example in the ban (in principle) in France on requests for a CV with photograph—to prevent their physical appearance from being a disadvantage to job candidates—and even in the idea of anonymous CVs, to prevent the a priori exclusion of candidates of foreign extraction; society is requested to submit to the economy, and to slide yourself into it you may even have to abandon your name. Even more worrying is the wish of some academics to equalize the grades of schools where (miraculously) French is spoken and written with those where having the Baccalauréat signifies neither knowledge of the rule of three nor the ability to write a word of French, all in the name of indeterminacy. At a polemical extreme lies the demand of some male homosexual couples to adopt and raise children, with or without marriage, thus freeing themselves from the so-called laws of nature, which once set the relation between the sexes as the basis of reproduction, but which they notice are everywhere flouted, and are probably now kept in existence only to oppose their wish!

Wrinkles used to indicate age and what it brings. White hair, slower and more measured movements, used to express the passage of time. Wrinkles, white hair and slow movements are what we no longer want to see, what ought to disappear from the far end of life. A whole panoply of tints and dyes, hair implants, anti-age serums, anti-ageing creams, anti-first-signs-of-ageing creams, face-masks and exfoliations, vitaminized products and adapted hormones are available and used, before surgery is even mentioned. One in six Frenchmen over 60 has considered resorting to cosmetic surgery, and one in a hundred has actually done so. The shift is in both directions: old age is setting in later and later, but—or should that be because?—its effects are actively resisted earlier and earlier. The average age of the first facelift has dropped from 50 to 41. Treatment of signs of ageing—wrinkles, loss of skin tone and so on—starts at 30. Anxiety is seizing the body. And it may be that the relentless effort to vanquish time, which has doubled sales of anti-ageing products in four years, reveals the final project: to extract time itself from the human body, and give it immortality.

This rejection is fundamental. Whether stated as a sole principle by business managers and recruitment consultancies, featured in the explicit and implicit codes of TV networks, newspapers and journals, whether it is written into the law or the rules adopted by private companies short of managerial nous, rejection of any determination other than by individual will is essential to the process of inventing the body. Debated in the European parliament in June 2004, the European Commission's wish to ban any difference in premiums based on the sex of the insured, in car insurance as well as in life insurance contracts, even though such differences generally favour women (who smoke less, drink less, drive more cautiously and take fewer risks), means the dismissal of reality in the name of overruling nature. Because it rejects what nature gives as well as what it withholds. Because it asserts that life is plastic; that everyone can fill the role he wants to play, with the support of the law and public money, in defiance of what he is, where he comes from and what he can do. And it designates a desperate flight from the specific; from all that used to be specific to the human species, rootedness, attachment, heritage, belonging, all now required to give way to the radiant sun of the indeterminate, endlessly restless, flexible and detached ego.

The body, that one and only body, has to be so carefully underwritten, maintained, protected, fulfilled according to its choices and wishes that in the end it has to be produced from the ground up, with nothing left to chance, in every way and at all costs. New publications in history, criticism, law, are working towards marshalling the works and deeds of the past into line with this requirement of indeterminacy … playing down anything resembling victory, vengeful passion, thirst for blood; and playing down too anything that encourages pride in the self, that confirms identity or deciphers origin. Like Walt Disney Studios producing images of asexual animals—lions and stags with censored genitals, eunuch kings—the US is setting the example with software programs designed to purge art works (books, films, plays, interviews) of words, scenes and situations that might upset today's audiences, censoring in the process the Bible, the Koran and the works of Racine, Shakespeare and many others. The staging of a Mozart opera, *Idomeneus*, which includes a representation of the Prophet Muhammad considered ironic and offensive, was banned in the winter of 2007 following pressure from Muslim clerics. Falsifying the world itself counts for less than censoring its representation; better to suppress reality, which is always incorrect, and substitute its representation, which can always be made to toe the line. The zero-risk hypothesis is coming true little by little, in that patient and systematic machining of the world to make it fit the rules and submit to the law, thus adapting it to the market: fluid, slick, without sharp edges or big words. And we are all expecting it to come true in the distancing of the human species from the curses of illness, suffering and accident. Nothing human is ever again to escape from the fields of law, volition and knowledge. That tacit wish underlies the new common attitude to suffering, beauty, desire and fulfilment.

The end of nature

> In the spring of 2005, warnings were issued to the public in the Aveyron advising people to be on their guard against the risks of respiratory and skin disorders caused by pollen from cypress trees, wild flowers and orchards. One could not help wondering why the politicians responsible had failed to remedy the situation. And what on earth were the police doing about it?

Of course in this society, wholly bent on eliminating it, nature—as representation, as offering, as myth—is everywhere. It is no longer natural, but it is still naturizing. The addition to the preamble of the French Constitution decided in May 2004, of a precautionary principle raised to the status of universal rule, for the first time placed a principle of constitutional import under the sign of naturalism. But what nature is meant exactly? In entering the domain of law, that nature has changed. It is replaced by its idea. Its representation satisfies us. The obsessive figure of a desired, fantasized, idealized Nature is replacing nature as life, as land, as system, as truth ... we are living through the end of nature at a time when its reconstitution is becoming more real than its protection, and its representation more abundant than its reality. Human labour was supposed to vanquish nature, to clear, drain and contain it, inaugurating the world of humans; in an exhausted world, human labour is going to have to remake, from nature's remains, its copy or synthesis. It is worth noting too that while bewailing its disappearance with increasing vehemence, we continue to employ all means to hasten, to organize that disappearance, so unbearable has nature become, so impossible for new men like ourselves to accommodate; so content are we with its representation alone. We have to bury it, even before it stops moving, so that we can dance at luxurious length in front of the myth it will have become.

What does 'natural landscape' mean on French or European soil? Natural species, when thousands of local varieties of plants and farm animals are vanishing and being replaced by a few dozen varieties fabricated for their profitability? Land, when thousands of hectares of greenhouses, models of soil-free cultivation, are making Dutch flower-growers and Breton vegetable producers rich, and are going to win Eastern Europe over to crops freed by investment from the local climatic, geological and hydrological conditions? And what will 'geography' mean in a few years' time, with Dubai building dream suburbs on dozens of artificial islands in the Gulf, while fish farms are colonizing hundreds of miles of coastline in Asia and the Pacific? What can possibly survive of nature when the frenzy of evangelist missionaries, sects and teachers joins with the wishes of landowners, the schemes of oil majors and satellite-dish peddlers, to liquidate the surviving fringes of what we call civilization, and bring them under the norms of desire and consumption? Nature henceforth is nowhere independent of man, his choices, his processes, and nowhere does it depend on anything but his volition, conscious or not. The Westerner is achieving the indeterminacy he seeks by first making nature and geography dependent on him, then neglecting them. Names like 'nature reserve', 'wildlife park' and so on proliferate, while the reality they overlay steadily dissolves. On the scale of countries, or continents, only the Antarctic is protected from industrial exploitation—but for how long?—by international agreement. No agreement saved the North Atlantic from overfishing, and the near-disappearance of resources thought everlasting, foremost among them the Newfoundland cod, is explosively emblematic, and underlined by the sad litany of deserted quays, rotting lobster pots and decaying trawlers that stretches from Labrador to Saint-Pierre, from Port-aux-Basques to Blanc-Sablons.

It may not be the end of history, but it ought to be the end of an artifice, a pretension; nature is no more, will never again be more than a convention, and any invocation of the nature of things will betray the purpose of its author: a hidden purpose, an unadmitted pretension. Our reality henceforth is the product of industry, technology and human reason. The most immediate form of otherness, that is what is lost when nature goes away. Nature, like living in the wild, has entered the domain of choice, value and the market, being already in that of private property, and thus of the rarity sanctioned and produced by it. There is nothing external to us any more; nothing we are not responsible for now. The world is small, nature is scarce, and anyone who can pay the price can incorporate it into the field of production; behind the general disquiet on climate change, urban pollution and the alleged decline of living conditions, it is hard not to discern a nascent wish to control temperatures, rainfall, sunlight ... and air quality of course. And behind the surprising anxiety and distress now affecting Europe, one cannot help feeling the mounting fear inspired by a force with no purpose, a power with no master, an action without conscious direction.

Loss of the real

The problem is not that we have vanquished it, but that we have done away with it altogether. A victory so complete that it threatens the victor. With the disappearance of nature, what is occurring is a second death of God, of that modest everyday God who stated rules and laws confirmed as authoritative by the most humble and immediate human experience, and praised as harmonious in school-certificate science ... because ponds fill, because apples fall, because you can measure a mile and a half on foot, and if two trains leave in opposite directions at the same time... It is those rules, those laws and the dependable tangible landmarks in space and time that they provide, that are wavering and should be distrusted. The natural has become the enemy; so, wrong. The real, that is what is leaving us. Not only because of those masters of suspicion, second only to analysts, the scientists of relativity, the expanding universe, chaos theory or genetics.

Because of the speed which is redrawing all maps, gigabytes that dwarf human memory, networks that abolish time (or purport to); and because of our mastery of fertility, of pain, of sickness and death (why not?), all the categories of perceptible experience that used to mediate the relation between our bodies and the outside world have been overturned: distance is measured in hours by aircraft, train or car, not in miles, and reality comes in pixels or bytes. This has occurred all at once, in every area and all directions, without a learning period for the world and states of the body to adapt to the change being possible, or being consciously sought.[2]

Yes, this is about the disappearance of another God, dispenser of rules from elsewhere that apply to all, the God of the real. A modest God, terribly efficient in his job, which is to remind people where their limits are and of their participation in a common world, the empire of the laws of nature. Everyday existence used to be under the dominion of the sacred because the body came up against its own limits all the time; technical conditioning of the real, the natural, is destroying this dominion by pushing back those limits. Our experiences of the world condemn that God. The need for religion and the sacred, and the need for nature, are still there. But it is risky to read into that a return of the religious, a protection of nature, a rebirth of the sacred. We will have ersatz equivalents. Rave dances with their techno, house and trance music can fulfil their devotees in a manner resembling quite closely what was once the preserve of the sacred; well-managed parks give quite intense impressions of nature by showcasing its scenery and cues; but these are not the sacred or nature, they are substitutes. They compensate for a liquidation that is nearly complete, one that answers almost none of the few questions it poses. For this liquidation liquidates the question too. It is not the departure, the removal, of something that would then be missed, or in any case need to be replaced; it is a fading away for lack of interest, a progressive deficiency, a gradual erasure of raisons d'être. The old question—how to replace what has been done away with—is pointless here. The society of the body has no need to replace religion, the sacred, nature, because the society of the market with which it is entangled is very good at producing social functions and states of the body—excitement, vibration, communion—that are sufficient in themselves: it is done by the culture industry.

---

2. But is the departure from nature setting the scene for a return to nature, perhaps signalled by the fashion for alternative medicine, biotechnologies and biomedicines? See Alan Peterson, *The Body in Question*, Routledge, 2006.

End of the sacred?

The end of nature, the end of the body as terrain, as uncertainty, as a condition, is revealed in its true light: the elimination of all reference to a law from on high or from elsewhere that would not obey our choices, the disappearance of chance events or destiny from what forms the framework of life, and from life itself. Everything that happens happens on screen, and nowhere else is as real as that, or in any case more real. The resulting extension of the market is an aspect of the new conquest under way. For its primary terrain is the human body. In the abyss behind the surpassing of nature through its representation, we can discern the invention of the body through its production. Perhaps the one needs to complete its disappearance altogether before the other can be wholly free of its law, and perhaps the primary gamble of the end of nature is the end of the body as we know it, the end of the body as it still reproduces, grows, lives and dies today. For what lives and what still speaks of nature in the body will soon be reduced to silence, like fate, like memory, like regret.

In just a few years, a number of frontiers have fallen after having been in place for centuries—starting with the interdict on voluntary modifications to the body, a matter pronounced on by the religions of the Book, the sense of the sacred and analysis among other authorities: it has been shaken by recent strides in cosmetic surgery as well as modern wonders of implantation and grafting. Followed by the species barrier: cows contracted BSE when they were made carnivorous. Specialized production houses offer a full catalogue of films depicting relations between men or women and a whole selected zoo, of donkeys, apes, dogs, snakes ... only Leda and the Swan are still missing, but that gap will soon be filled no doubt by imaginative Asian and East European producers, rich with Hellenic culture. On a more serious level, the species barrier is transgressed in the transplantation to humans of organs and tissue taken from animals, usually pigs, a technology that seems to have a good future at least while the cultivation of organ-donor clones remains banned and unpredictable.

Indeed, the indeterminacy of frontiers with the animal world seems to be just as important as indeterminacy between the sexes. Animals used to be menacing, or instrumentalized, or prey. Now they are becoming our fellows. A millennial barrier is breaking down, not just with the multiplication of pet animals or the appetite for wildlife as a spectacle, but with the fact that cruelty to animals is frowned on as slavery once was, that there are more and more vegetarians, and that an international movement in favour of animal rights is developing ... a different sign of the end of nature. Otherness is at stake. The Darwinian view, placing the human species over all the others, as a final outcome, is refuted; the earthworm is a final outcome too, like the nightingale. The human species has the specificity that it can kill all the others, but that is not permitted on pain of destroying itself. An old order of value has been overturned; it becomes more obvious every year that the destruction of the surviving members of threatened species is a crime as grave as crimes once committed against human beings, that the destruction of natural species is also, in a different way, a crime against humanity. How many Europeans these days, on seeing a picture of a Congolese soldier laughing over the corpse of a freshly killed mountain gorilla, feel more sympathy for the ape than the man? The end of humanism too perhaps, in the lucid and urgent transfer from a situation where the world as nature was given, to a situation where it is chosen. Professor Yves Christen approaches the question by asking whether it is possible to trace a dividing line between the human and the animal, on the basis of observed facts, that confirms all that we thought we knew about the difference. 'There is nothing specific to humanity', he concludes. 'More precisely, the genetic and epigenetic characteristics that distinguish us from the other species do not make us superior. In the great game of selection, those that have survived win over those that have died out, without any hierarchy being apparent.'[3]

Body prostheses

It is an exploration that has hardly begun, a different way of being with this designed, produced, enriched, improved, fully equipped body. The body has become used to prostheses that have liberated it from memory, that detach it from time and space, that modify the terms of presence, of distance and action. And it has adapted itself to these tools that used to spare it from effort, fatigue or risk, and that now spare it from having to learn or remember, analyse or discern, foresee or conceive. Use of the memory, the senses, the mind, has been modified by the television

3. Yves Christen, *L'Animal est-il une personne?* (Are animals people?), Flammarion, 2009.

screen, the computer memory, the credit card. A new way of thinking, of knowing, of seeing oneself, has emerged from that; and the omnipresent demand for reflexivity is both multiplied and overturned by the internet, by webcams and digital photos; because to see oneself is to exist, and because everyone is first of all his own producer, witness and Peeping Tom. New ways of relating to others, of knowing, reflecting, finding information, arguing, consuming, paying, appear as a result. In the end a whole new way of being emerges. For as these prostheses become more indispensable, more integral, more familiar, they come to identify us, a little like the mobile phones that, hanging round the neck on a cord or brandished in one hand, are marks of identity and distinction among the dancers in Moscow discothèques. And with the confusion of functions and the implantation of terminals in the body itself, what emerges really is a different way of relating to things, to others and the self. The integration of photography, followed by video, into the mobile phone forms an intelligent terminal providing sound and moving image, able to receive messages from outside, reproduce them, and digitalize external material to broadcast them in its turn. The addition of wi-fi internet access opens this terminal to the field of memory, libraries and data banks, delegating to it the functions of wisdom and knowledge. The next stage could integrate payment facilities with the terminal, so that all communication with the outside world involving sound, image, numbers or the written word will be concentrated in it. And the stage after that—which promises to see the integration of different functions of the terminal into the body itself, wiring them into the nervous system via subcutaneous chips, in parallel with the extraordinary effects of the use of nanotechnologies for medical, sporting or pleasure purposes—announces a further evolution, one that is going to complement the senses and the mind. It is not out of place to see it as imposing new constraints, notably those being forced on spoken tongues by the language of the computer, the internet, SMS and chatrooms, replacing them with newspeak forms. It is not out of place to see a danger of sliding into something post-human, something humanoid, already being predicted for the mid-century by some nanotechnology zealots. It is not out of place to recognize the unprecedented constraints through the body that these new media impose: the Goncourt brothers were impressed to learn that the ladies-in-waiting at the British Court took a daily enema to ensure that no physical need would interfere with their duties (Goncourts' journal, 1864); Degas took against the telephone, which enabled anyone to 'ring for me like a domestic'; we have abandoned such attitudes and established a permanent unlimited availability, making a switched-off mobile a moral slip and the failure to answer emails every day the equivalent of a driving offence (it is true of course that an office worker today probably has lower self-esteem than a lady-in-waiting to the Queen of England in the 1860s). Most of all, it is necessary to recognize the unprecedented extension it gives to the possibilities of imagination, of discovery and sensation, that will be multiplied when the senses and the mind are freed from the mechanical tasks of memory, classification and analysis, and written or spoken expression. Permanence, ubiquity, reversibility; a few of the categories of human experience are being overturned, and are going to fabricate a new earthly condition. To speak, to write, to learn, will not have the same universal meanings; they will fall under the sway of discrimination and separation.

After all these transgressions, their spread and multiplication, what we are witnessing really is the end of the body as we have known it, as it has been received, protected and transmitted. To counter destiny—whether of land, race, climate or the gods—nothing surely would be too much, and in fact nothing is too much today. So that, faced with the human body, with nature, or what exists in its place, the task now is not so much to deal with the consequences of their exhaustion, considerable attrition being already apparent, as to organize the conditions for their replacement. So that the driving objective of the economy is now to bring the body, nature, which turns out to be in short supply, under the dominion of choice, investment, production and the market.

Nature has to be produced because it is in short supply, and because it threatens at all times to disappoint consumer expectations either by vanishing or by grossly exceeding them.

And the body has to be produced to stop it from evading choice, to bring it into history—in other words into progress, into its methods and technology—and to make it keep all life's promises, converted into assurances and rights.

Production of life

A young Frenchwoman, a graduate of Essec (École supérieure des sciences économiques et commerciales), won the Harvard Business School's prize for the most innovative project in June 2004. Her suggestion was to start a company in Boston to preserve the ova of young unmarried women (there

> are five million in the US aged between 20 and 27 who delay childbearing in order to pursue their professional careers) to enable them to conceive at the time of their choice (usually in their forties) under the best possible conditions (after the age of 27, the quality of the ovum declines). She evaluates the market as being worth several tens of millions of dollars annually, with several hundred thousand potential clients.
>
> In Belgium, where fertilization of a woman by an external donor is almost completely liberalized, a young male AIDS sufferer nominated his own father as a sperm donor to conceive his son. Belgian doctors saw no problem in successfully carrying out a procedure that made a father his son's brother … did someone mention the incest taboo?

Something is changing in the mode of human reproduction and in the relation between work, age and the wish for a child. A disjunction is taking place in US society that involves the place of the child in life. Eighty per cent of mothers aged 15 to 19 at the birth of their first child are African-American; 80 per cent of women bearing children after the age of 45 are white…

When Craig Venter, who pioneered the deciphering of the human genome, can successfully reassemble the Meccano of life from a virus to a bacterium; when the advancing technology of extra-uterine embryo culture using an artificial uterus (ectogenesis) promises the development of embryo farms in the near future; when medically assisted parents are described (by a Paris research centre) as 'partners in the creation of a child'; when women auction their services as surrogate mothers on the internet (in early 2005, exploiting loopholes in the Belgian law); when a mother planning a child is in a position to bid for gametes determining some of the child's major characteristics (offered by Ron's Angels) and to select its genetic quotient; when it is possible, or soon will be, to eliminate in advance from a child's makeup any 'leprous' genomes, so called because they carry a tendency to particularly serious illnesses (haemophilia, cancers, asthma, Alzheimer's, Huntington's Chorea, muscular dystrophy, diabetes …); when future management of health insurance depends to a notable extent on the capacity to conceive and bear children protected against any hereditary illness or defect, and thus on the elimination of the most serious and expensive illnesses; when all these things are with us, only an error of vocabulary can explain why the word 'reproduction' is still applied to the human species, in the way it is applied to animal species in the wild.

Birth under control

The society of the market is reinventing the distinction that antiquity observed between the natural phenomenon of birth and the social recognition of the child. India and China, where female children are sometimes done away with, are reinventing the Roman practice of exposing children not accepted by the head of the family; while French law, considering a pregnant woman a fragile individual, and taking the decision on whether to have a child liable to grave pathologies out of her hands (giving it instead to doctors and doctors alone), is embarking on a new social control of the right to life. When mothers can carry a child which is genetically unrelated both to them and the man they have chosen to be its father, a child which one day will know the conditions of its birth (starting as a spare embryo in the storage freezer of an assisted procreation centre, and having the good luck to be chosen to carry out the parenting project of a sterile couple) but will not have the right or the ability to discover its biological parents, only by abusing language is it still possible to use words like parents, maternity and paternity. The anonymous donation of the embryo dissociates biological from juridical parenthood. Contraception, abortion and divorce practice are dismissing men from procreation and are close to awarding women a parenting monopoly; 250,000 frozen embryos are awaiting surrogate mothers in the first body supermarkets. Myths concerning birth, myths of the self, myths of origin, of the Father and the Name, multiplied for millennia before the role of the man–woman relation was admitted; the conditions are now present for the appearance of new myths of birth, making the body into a product, an advance, a technology.

Despite the vaunted rigour of the French law on bioethics, voted in 1993 and amended in 2003, via the restricted, but widened, tolerance of therapeutic abortion, and via the progressive extension of diagnostics and tests on the child in the womb, and despite vigorous debate in the US, slippage has occurred in a millennial order. Breakthroughs in therapeutic cloning make it clear that sooner or later France will have to overcome its backwardness and catch up. How could it be otherwise, when couples frustrated in their desire for a child only have to take the Eurostar or cross the line that used to mark the Belgian border to find the answers they want? Nature's choice is giving way constantly to human decision. Who will complain, when the promise to rid the human species of the evils that have always afflicted it is about to be kept? Before the end of this decade it will be possible to carry out 3,000 to 5,000 tests fairly cheaply (a few hundred dollars for the whole set) on the genetic code (DNA) of the child in the womb, using specialized chips, to measure any gap between the embryo's genetic morbidity quotient and the average for the whole population. The combination of in-vitro fertilization and genetic screening brings the management of a population's health quality a step closer. The explosion that started in 1990 with the creation of a public consortium to finance the deciphering of the human genome, resulting in tens of thousands of patent applications covering more than 30,000 genes in 2003, is ending with the scientific wish to read the human heritage (and to interfere with it) finding a place in the world of merchandise, the contract and the market. It is obvious that developed countries, confronted with explosive growth in health expenditure and the resulting unsustainable deficits, are going to start thinking about the health capital of their citizens and considering all ways of forecasting, improving and strengthening the genetic capital of that population; not just to reduce expenditure on health, but to improve the population's performances and facilitate accurate planning. And it is equally obvious, surely, that developing countries, with high exposure to hereditary illnesses and endemic pathologies, are going to use all available means to shed the burden of hereditary defects, adult physical deficiencies and the curse of sickness, to concentrate all the forces of an immunized or protected population on growth and economic activity.

Sovereign motherhood

'A child if I want, when I want and how I want.' And now, 'the child I want'. Most women in developed societies have the children they choose to have. They are increasingly likely to have them when and how they choose to have them, conceived by whomever they choose for the purpose (or if necessary without any male involvement, for which medicine can effectively deputize); the symmetrical risks of unwanted births and sterility are diminishing with equal speed; conception has ceased to be subject to chance and entered the domain of technology and guaranteed benefits. Predictions that the next decade will see embryo or baby farms, whose products will be spared birth trauma by not having to make the effort of being born, or carrier fathers exempted from female involvement to give birth to a desired, programmed, chosen, implanted child (a technical possibility with profound implications for the debate on child adoption by homosexual couples), are not some medical student's fantasies but serious forecasts by specialists in the treatment of sterility. Heterosexual marriage already seems to be on its way out as the norm, to the advantage of the single parent—man or woman—raising the chosen child, at the chosen moment, conceived in the desired manner, in the setting he or she has chosen. Behind the production of bodies, it is parenthood that is being reinvented: as the choice of a child, therefore also as responsibility for the child. Or perhaps parenthood is disappearing ... for the child product of rational parental investment is invested with the duty of perfection; he or she ought to be perfect to live up to the wishes of the parents; to deserve the parents. Such is the coming drama: it will be up to children to deserve their parents, to justify the fact of having been born and the investment made to that end. The relation of the believer to God—giving thanks for having been chosen—is to be maintained by the child with each of his parents.

The connection between man–woman sexual relations and conception has lost any element of determination along with its mystery and unpredictability. Control over conception, starting with 'the pill' discovered in the sixties and legalized in France under the Neuwirth law of 1967, which prevented ovulation but only worked if taken regularly, extended in 1990 by the 'morning-after' pill that rescued women from fear of casual sexual encounters, has liberated women from the risk of unwanted pregnancy. That is a first stage; the next ones are already apparent here and there: choice of the child's sex; artificial insemination to overcome mechanical causes of sterility; measurement of the foetus's predispositions, to help decide whether or not to allow it to come to term; selection of genetic characteristics from sperm or ovum banks, etc. At variable but affordable rates, US and Israeli companies are already offering insemination with sperm from donors selected for intelligence, physique or both, at quite modest prices (from a few hundred to two thousand dollars in the case of Fairfax Cryobank's 2005 catalogue). That too is just a stage, and the rapidly increasing turnover and activity in animal cloning hints at what is coming next. Synthesizing biology promises nothing less than a usable living Meccano (either from stem cells taken from frozen umbilical cord, or from a cloned twin of every living human, a copy made at birth and grown without a brain to provide a lifelong supply of spare parts and tissues), comprising different parts capable of being assembled into living tissue at will, human, bacterial, viral or enzyme. Whatever the assurances given by institutes or the researchers themselves, the proliferation of firms and the concentration of capital on these projects in California and Israel, India and Japan, show how high the financial and industrial stakes are in developing the products of these technologies commercially, and extending their field of application to high added value products … and where but in man is the highest added value to be found?

Taken all together these innovations, some already being industrialized, will put an end to reproduction; children are going to be *produced* now, in every sense of the word: technical mastery, specific choice, and the market, with the cost-effectiveness it implies. The child is its mother's product. There will be no more accidental children, which also means that no more children will result from the love of a man and a woman; passion is sidelined; every child will result from the desire for a child, every child be the result of its mother's wish for it, the father being relegated to subordinate rank and any wish on his part being perhaps sympathetic, but inessential. Every child is the result of a wish, one that has yet to be scrutinized: a wish for what? A wish to keep on going through someone else? To consume the child as others consume travel? A wish for new experience, for a source of moral satisfaction? The adoption market, with its increasing consumption of children from poor countries—who are saved by adoption from a miserable fate—is the latest craze of nouveau-riche Americans and Europeans, and marks a further step in the dissociation between biological parentage, ethnic origin and economic and social parentage (the use of terms like 'affective parenting' calls for scrutiny at least). In fact a lot of examples from Hollywood and elsewhere seem to show that it is thought far smarter and more 'real' to go looking for one's child in some refugee camp or prairie at the back of beyond than in the local orphanage. The 'wish for a child' is a phrase that trips easily off the tongue; really though it is child consumption that our society has made into a value, a parenthood benefit that our society provides under the best conditions and that is celebrated competitively, as the growth market for fashionable and expensive children's clothes illustrates. The recent adoption fashion, which conveniently substitutes mercantile, administrative parenthood for biological parenthood, with its choices, its catalogues, its procedures, its price, embodies this production of parenthood. And behind the endless extension of the myth of the child, its spectacle, its desire, its purity, should we discern the disappearance of parents, of the capacity for letting go, for trust and giving, that used to be what being a parent meant?

In a significant shift of vocabulary, the expression 'make a child' is coming almost everywhere to replace 'have a child', at a time when sterility treatment is far from successful in all cases, at a time too when male sterility seems to be spreading quite rapidly ... what does that matter, when it is being denied that nature has anything at all to do with the choice, the free choice of a free woman! The choice of words suggests a production that medicine, or industry, cannot yet guarantee altogether. But men no longer reproduce themselves like natural beings under the sign of chance, luck or fate; women produce other men, and they decide what men to produce, first in number, then in qualities and personality, after procedures, choices and services one of whose apparent characteristics is that they are increasingly responsive to rules of investment, or whim. And instead of the family, we should perhaps think of the 'femily'; and recognize that the necessity to become a man, to scrutinize the self and invent a body, a gender, a mode of relation—a requirement until recently the millennial curse of women—now weighs on men whose role is no longer preordained anywhere; you are no longer born a man, you have to become one. So that a new differentiation of the sexes is taking shape, in this revolution in private life that confronts men for the first time with a social, sexual and family role that is not more or less preordained; and so that the notions of descent, of parentage and family, are having to be revised in the light of the solitary choice, common decision or shared whim that lies at the child's origin. But the element of spontaneity, of giving and chance, that used to be contained in the transmission of life is in danger of being lost on the cutting edges of technology and the market. And lastly, the quest for indeterminacy is being accompanied by the most unheard-of and problematic determination imaginable, the one making the child the object of its mother's choice, so far for financial reasons, tomorrow no doubt under the constraint of public order, that of the standardization of bodies to be born, and the law on bodies to be born, under the aegis of the good life and in the name of well-being.

A new economic continent

The first successful in vitro fertilization resulted in the birth of Louise Brown near Manchester on 25 July 1978. One couple in ten is seeking medical help for sterility in France; 110,000 births have taken place in

> France since 1982 as a result of medical assistance to procreation. The number of 'test-tube babies' was bound to increase with the propagation of sterility through deteriorating food quality, environment and living conditions; some pessimists are predicting that half of all couples in Europe will be sterile by 2050!

A birth, which used to be the word becoming flesh, is now a fund being invested. Bizarre or scandalous anecdotes concerning animal reproduction, from Dolly the sheep to the cloning of beloved pets (offered, for $30,000, since February 2002 by a company called Genetic Savings Clone), or the European Union's refusal to ratify the patent on a transgenic mouse in July 2004, are less significant than the transformation taking place at the same time in human reproduction.

The current demographic situation in developed countries, illustrating the strength of the so-called 'dinky' model, leaves no room for doubt. If the child can be chosen, if its characteristics can be determined, the moment of its birth specified and guaranteed, then no product can be more precious to its parents than it will be. If genetic technology makes it possible to spare a child from hereditary illnesses, premature disability, cancer as a young adult, cardiac weakness or respiratory insufficiency, if it eliminates the curse of death before the 'natural' life expectancy threshold, then who will hesitate to resort to it; who, indeed, would have the right to impose disability, hereditary defects or simple risks on their children by their own choice, the fruit of their convictions or simply some whim? A movement is under way, a movement mistrustful of life, seeking zero-risk options. In the name of the perfect child, it favours avoiding the risk of birth. In the name of parental responsibility, it conjures up the spectre of mental or physical disability, makes the child's handicap the moral fault of the parents, and in its own way validates the 'double income, no kids' model by making anxiety disappear under the dominion of a sterile sort of well-being.

Life and the norm

The arguments over eugenics, whether seen as positive (improving human stock by favouring births that allow a better quality of life, either through selective breeding or genetic manipulation) or negative (eliminating births presenting risks to the quality of life, notably through sterilization or preventive abortion), especially as they are being conducted in France, are broadly irrelevant to a relation that is becoming a market relation, and thus one of satisfaction. The body capable of a good life—capable of being satisfied with its life—ought to be born, and will soon be a possibility.

The spectacle of the good life, the life of fulfilled, sated, contented bodies, underlines the brutal transition between the right to life and the right of life. The clamour of opinions, the arbitrary nature of judgements and legislation, concerning the responsibility of scientists and researchers, is contributing to this transition. To a question presented as collective, requiring choices, decisions and legislation of a public nature, the responses are already (and will become increasingly) market responses, personal and arguable, with price as the final criterion. Insidious, subjective, but influenced by fashion and subject to manipulation, an individual eugenicism has emerged from the field of the possible and entered that of reality, in the first instance through the assessment of every unborn child's genetic endowment. The famous Perruche judgement—indemnifying a child born disabled following a prenatal diagnostic error, the mother having expressed a wish to abort if the foetus was abnormal, for the injury of having to live without benefit of its physical integrity—naively expressed the commonsense response to the quibbles of ethics professionals.[4] Those who take the responsibility of allowing the birth of a disabled child or one likely to develop an illness ought to deal with all the consequences of their choice, financial in particular; they cannot require society, which has provided them with the elements of that choice, to bear the consequences of their personal decision. Often disguised behind the notion of a 'parental project', or of the prevention of serious, incapacitating or disabling illnesses (Down's syndrome for example), recourse to all available techniques for prenatal diagnosis and genetic screening is destined to develop and to have broadly unforeseen consequences on saving and investment, on the finance and insurance industries, on consumption and on collective preferences. Defence of human cloning, notably in the form of brainless clones to supply spare organs, as presented by Professor Henri Atlan, embodies this reality;[5] whatever can be done against suffering, sickness and death will be done. It is our destiny. Since we are destined

4. The judgement did not become law as the right to be born was later enshrined in a law passed by the National Assembly, and the hundreds of thousands of euros awarded to the parents were reclaimed by the Social Security, against guaranteed healthcare for the child.

5. See Henri Atlan, *Le clonage humain*, Seuil, 1999.

to subject to our choice everything—private, affective, professional or economic—that we can.

The accounts of life

> An American woman obtains a grant to study at a US superfaculty. To get a housing loan, she has to undergo a genetic test. The test reveals the genes of a dormant illness that reduces her life expectancy. Cross-referencing enables the University to learn the results of the test, and leads it to withdraw the grant and award it to a student with better life expectancy, and no genetic risk of serious illness.

Life is a principal asset; and the return on that capital, in terms of anticipated revenue over time, deserves to be calculated, to optimize any investment decision. It is easy to denounce the US university's decision, but impossible to argue with its economic reasoning—better to invest in a student whose life expectancy is long—and quite difficult to deny that it offers a convincing picture of what is coming, anyway in this matter of assessing people's biological potential before employing them. Should an enterprise be required to bear the consequences of known chronic defects or illnesses? Optimizing the exploitation of that unique asset, the human body, is becoming a macro-economic and political subject. The genetic capital of a country, of a community, its capacity to prolong itself through time while minimizing its health expenditure and maximizing the performances of its members, can already be evaluated; soon it will become a determining factor for investor confidence, a measure of a society's attractiveness, its overall quality; so there will be pressure to generalize the available techniques, all of them, for improving the genetic quality of a population. No one would suppose that the superior level of health enjoyed by the French population, underlined by life expectancy that is among the world's highest, has no connection with the hourly productivity level of labour in France. A country or region whose population is well looked after, well fed, well educated in health matters, is more likely to grow, to be enterprising, to prosper. In a few years' time it will be necessary to add: and whose genetic capital is scientifically organized, managed and monitored.

The production of life promises to bring decisive breaks in some of the determining elements of the way people are themselves, and behave with their families and others. Impossible in France for reasons of 'political correctness'—all research focused on race being regarded there as politically delinquent and socially unthinkable—studies are actively pursued by the beauty industrialists who sell skin-lightening creams, hair straightener, etc., in North and South America and in Asia. The worldwide demand for such products leaves little room for doubt on the success of the offer that will sooner or later be made to parents to select, among other characteristics, the skin colour and racial type of their child-to-be. Socially ambitious families from Martinique and Guadeloupe, or Caribbean creoles, use the term 'bleaching'. What used to take place over the generations, through the alchemy of successive unions, will be ordered from a catalogue by choosing the genetic capital of the planned infant. The ultimate form of cross-breeding ... and might there not be a final solution to racial prejudice and discrimination, when the child has the skin colour its parents choose, when race is no longer necessarily the work of nature? No doubt; but the hidden preference of consumers may lead to the generalization of certain so-called 'Caucasian' features, white skin, blond hair, blue eyes, and ensure the permanence, even the universalization, of a model whose birth rate today appears to condemn it to disappearance. By way of the conception market, the great genetic bazaar could multiply as a product what is disappearing as part of nature: the prototype of Klaus Barbie, of Aragorn or Siegfried, universalized as a prized human format. A new economic model is making its appearance: the human beings market.

The mystery of the Incarnation is as central to Christian society as the technologized production of bodies will be in the new society; the break with modes of reproduction as they have always been, among the animal, vegetable and human species, will undoubtedly be as determining for the men and women to be born in the twenty-first century as was the appearance of Christianity, with its vision of a distant world of God, foreign to the human world, and different. The periods before and after the production of bodies will be seen as different eras; the difference speaks loudly of the vast foreignness of modern society to traditional societies. We are inventing a new way of making bodies. Incarnation will be under a different sign for future generations: the sign of technology, of indices and ratios. With birth removed from nature to become a matter of choice, it is not difficult to predict that death too will be removed from nature and become choice. That is the novelty that will dominate the historical condition of humanity in the decades to come. It will play a part in the appearance of a new economic continent, that of the production of bodies, in which life is summoned to the market from before its beginning until after its end.

The relations market

> Sex is treated as a secondary aspect of those important matters, sickness and power.
>
> Allan Bloom[6]

The advent of the body will thus have completed that part of the Western project called reason, measure or cost, and which is instituting a different form of power and control, control and power over life, by way of the market in human relations. It is difficult not to see this as a remarkable breakthrough in the liberal project of departing from nature into human self-determination. Transhumanism is under way, according to its Swedish founder Nick Bostrom, via steady technological improvement in the capacities of the human species.[7]

The dissociation of sexuality from reproduction is already complete; the pursuit of sexual satisfaction, with or without a sexual relationship, is becoming remote, probably forever, from the production of a child, after having freed itself from the risk of a child. The association of pleasure and life, that couple that passed on its determining forms to human relations and gave apparent permanence to the human condition, has been severed. Firstly because the HIV virus violently replaced it with an association of pleasure with death. Then because the market set itself up as the common denominator between pleasure and life. From another point of view, what used to exist as part of nature, as a drive and a gift, is being presented as a product, a service, with a price. Far from ending in 'free' sexual relations, the alleged liberation is bringing into the market a domain that used to be free. The success on the internet of computer-assisted sex has been dazzling. Sales of products and services in this area on the net represent between 6 and 10 per cent of total electronic business turnover. It is an exemplary substitute for physical relations and emotion, a type of sexual consummation whose economics—solitary and abundant, but impoverished, undifferentiated and obsessive—opens a hitherto unknown space

6. Allan Bloom, *Amour et Amitié*, Edition de Fallois, 1996.

7. But that achievement raises as many questions as it answers; to understand this see notably, in the abundant literature on risk, Alan Peterson's *Health, Risk and Vulnerability*, Routledge, 2007.

for unsatisfied desire, one that will be further enlarged by the appearance of nanotechnologies, or more precisely neuro-nano-biotechnologies. The American sociologist James Hugue predicts for the mid twenty-first century 'a sexuality without physical contact and without a partner ... through the use of nano-, neuro- and biotechnological interfaces'.[8] Animation in Western society is increasingly organized around the massive, consensual, systematic representation of sexual matters as a trade, service and market. Having sex with another person will make society when nothing else does any longer.

But for how long? The ceaselessly growing gap between sexual exchange and procreation will not be the means to a hitherto unknown sexual freedom for long; it can just as easily become the means to a new prohibition, of which the US is setting an example at this moment, and whose probable direction is indicated by some of the behaviour of young French women and men. The prohibition will be less moral than mercantile, opening wide the space of satisfactions at set prices and commercial services. For those at least who lack the good fortune or the means to form stable, exclusive and unpaid—in other words, trusting—relationships, sexuality becomes virtual, onanistic and paid for; the norm is replaced by the credit card number; anything that can be done can be bought; and with any relationship excluded, commitment is out of place. The number of adolescents sexually blocked by the need for sexual performance and the obsession with unattainable technique to guarantee mutual satisfaction lends conviction to the idea of a quest for satisfaction without sexual exchange, of a generalized autosatisfaction in which the other becomes so similar to the self, and at the same time so untouchable, that relations with him or her are excluded. The spread of shops specializing in feminine sexual accessories, initiated in Paris (in an annexe to a clothes shop) by the Sonia Rykiel brand, suggests not the normalization of a private practice, but the public recognition of a normalized practice. With less desire, but more guaranteed satisfaction: what the specialist magazines call a new way of approaching sexuality, in all delicacy and conviviality, in solitude and an inability to relate. The quest for indeterminacy reaches an ultimate level when it leads people to do without the other. The new forms of celibacy, whether resulting from a choice made in youth or following some separation later in life, help fill out the picture of a liberation pushed to the

8. Cited in *Libération*, 18 March 2008.

point of occluding actual relations; to the enduring relational desert that the exclusive satisfaction of the self is preparing.

The production of bodies

> The history of bodies as models, as morality and an ideal, is worth spelling out. In this history, so-called 'erotic' films, exemplified by the iconic figures of Brigitte Bardot and Roger Vadim, and then 'X' films from 1974 onward, took over from war films, broad social epics, then love stories; the bodies of specialist actresses and actors took the place that heroes, pioneers and lovers occupied before them as mirror and ideal. The reality of naked bodies, from total depilation in the 1990s to the generalization of surgery to enhance breasts and sex organs around 2000, tells the story of a transformation which is also an advent: an advent of the market in bodies, of the fabrication of bodies as a satisfaction technique, of the standardization of bodies as a condition of salvation, a means to endless desire and a capitulation to the new morality of the good life.

Health used to be subject to chance, or in the hands of the gods. Allah, Jesus, the ancestors or the river god conferred on their chosen ones the long, very long lives that no human knowledge or technique could guarantee. Hence the respect, the veneration even, given to those whose great age was the visible mark of special protection from the beyond, because they had survived or escaped the serious injuries or illnesses that killed everyone else. The Samburu, nomad pastoralists who live on the banks of Lake Turkana, call their elders 'the survivors': those who have gone over to the other side of life. And a Samburu today becomes an elder at 40, as his ancestors did five centuries ago. Hence too the respect attached to the body, that even today makes suicide a crime in British common law, that fills the witness of deliberate mutilations with horror, that clothes the fantasized repression of masturbation, female and male, and keeps sadomasochism, whether theatrical or bloody, among the rare sexual practices still defying interdiction. The economics of the body were enshrined in law; a French colonel used to parade his troops, weapons reversed, past the corpse of every suicide, flung on the stable dung heap. Expenditure of the body was the prime object of government; and control of the man's body for war, the woman's for childbearing, the progenitor of all victories.

Until the twentieth century, life was governed by the machine of the body under the auspices of wear, illness and age. Being born, loving, suffering, dying, stayed the same over so many millennia! The hazards of medicine, confidence in its progress and techniques, gratitude to practitioners, dominated a relation to health in which suffering remained a close companion, illness a familiar fear, death an ever-present eventuality … and a cure a piece of luck to be celebrated, the opposite of a right. 'I wish you the best of health.' The traditional courtesy was meant to ward off fate, and was a different expression of the very ancient and very familiar 'May the gods, (or God) bless you!' Health was what resisted illness and overcame it, in the sight of death, as a temporary respite or piece of luck. Medicine was primarily attention, compassion, giving comfort before achieving, sometimes, a cure; and no doubt sometimes, happily, it cured the patient, rather than his or her illness against which it was all too often powerless. Rather than providing a cure, it helped the patient to cure himself, if he could, in any way he could. In Western medicine, close in this respect to many other human societies, the magical figure of the physician was the centrepiece of the patient's expectations, the patient being a version of the child who is told: The doctor's coming! Technique now aspires to replace him. Our health systems have engendered systems for curing rather than giving care—an aftermarket physical repair industry rather than a public health service—and are organizing the material conditions for the recognition of a right to health, which magistrates will translate into judgements.

The shift in emphasis from healing/curing to the imperative of a flattering self-image, satisfaction with the self and pleasure in being, has changed everything. Everything is different now that L'Oréal, Danone, the full caddies of vitamin-supplement capsules in the healthfood shop or the week of Thalassotherapy are replacing the family doctor (or the analyst's couch). And everything has changed now that the obligation to be active to work and make a living, then the wish to stay young and attractive to please others and form relationships, have been succeeded by the obsession with feeling fit and well, liking one's own image and giving oneself pleasure. It is as if the objective criteria of health had gradually dissolved into an all-embracing concept of physical, mental and moral well-being, filling the shelves of bookshops with a mass of what might be called art-of-living texts, manuals of etiquette and stylish living, that might be summed up as dealing with what people owe to themselves; so that people now devote to the art of living with themselves what they used to devote to ways of getting on with others; so that self-reflexivity makes every individual his own producer/director, his own eavesdropping audience, generalizing telereality with everyone his own star on his own screen. Consumption of tranquillizers and other pharmaceutical products, and of soothing, conformist societal values, thus share in the same quest for well-being. The mind must be at peace that the body may exult. Virtue is good for repose and digestion.

For the first time, we are faced with a humanity that is really separated: by bodies, in other words by suffering and death. Broken, decayed teeth, worn, limping or crippled bodies, wrinkles and scars, separate the worlds more than money. Lovely woman friend with your ivory smile, what civilizations separate you from those others and their gap-toothed grinning gums! My living space, my physical condition, separate me from the Mumbai beggar more surely than the thick wodges of rupees in my pocket. In the Marrakesh palm-grove where I was jogging that morning in 2002, years of patient and measured training carried me past the teenage cyclists who had been cheering me on with a mocking glint in their eyes (as Gide's small boys must have done). And what a world separates the bikini-clad Israeli at Eilat from her veiled Palestinian contemporary, already a mother of ten, in the camp at Jenin! The human species is less united by a common fate in terms of birth, suffering and death than radically separated by different ways of being born, not suffering and making a discreet exit. And this inequality between humans has a meaning it has never had before since the dawn of humanity: a different presence of nature in the way of being born, growing and dying. The metamorphosis of our European bodies is being achieved at the cost of an unprecedented break with the bodies of others; of the majority. Eight hundred million in these bodies, four billion in those. What can we ever know of those bodies we understand only through the illusion of language, as if suffering, death and fear could be understood too! The availability worldwide of tall, blonde Barbie dolls, dolls of Claudia Schiffer, testifies to the globalization of the Western body. Now other bodies are being globalized with the appearance of Asian, African and Pacific Barbies. 'People from the North are becoming a clear minority on our planet,' wrote Ryszard Kapuściński.[9] The bodies that used to be here are not the ones that will be here in future. We are entering a different history of bodies, in which Western ethnocentrism will give way to a culture, representations, perhaps a civilization based on a very different body… but which?

9. In *Ebène*, Plon, 2000.

The transformation market

> For porn stars, professionals in X-rated products, as for the women and men who pose for photographers or strut the fashion catwalk, fine-tuning is not restricted to the garments worn for the occasion: the body, too, is increasingly often tweaked. Like Guy Bourdin contorting the bodies of his models to obtain surreal shapes, more and more producers, directors and photographers are requiring models to readjust some aspect of their bodies, some measurement not quite up to specification. These professional requirements are becoming a style. Almost a million North American women have chosen to undergo three or more serious cosmetic operations over the last ten years: changed their bodies three times within a decade. Large breasts, small breasts; pouting bee-stung lips or fine-drawn rosebud mouth … fashion has reached the body.

Saudi princesses, Kuwaiti oil sheikhs, monarchs of stage and screen, all know that London is the place for eye operations, although Tiger Woods and a select group of American billionaires have followed US Air Force pilots to Switzerland for a laser operation on their corneas to double their visual acuity. The Syrian president Bashir al-Assad, like Nelson Mandela, knows that Paris is the capital of cardiac care and some prostheses; King Hussein of Jordan knew that American clinics are unequalled in treating cancers (except in France perhaps); but Brazil has the best cosmetic surgery, Thailand is the place for sex-change clinics, while in Italy and California master sorcerers defy all the rhythms of natural life to enable women in their fifties to conceive for the first time. In 2005 a Romanian woman of 66 gave premature birth to a child weighing three and a half pounds; how long will that record stand? Of the 36 million occasional sportsmen and women in France, six million take part in some form of competition, and around 6,000 of those are listed as 'high-level' athletes. A significant proportion of this group is already chemically enhanced, and genetic enhancement will not be far behind. All doping apart, they will benefit from tissue engineering to ensure joints that are permanently supple or regenerate instantly, exceptionally short recovery periods, unfailing concentration and nervous control, sharpened specialization of musculature and tendons … specified by whom? Some trainers, working on programmes to produce world records or Olympic champions in ten years' time, are already counting on the embryonic stem cell cultures being developed at ten universities to replace defective organs (four universities in the US, two in India, two in Israel, one in Sweden and one in Australia have human stem cell lineages approved by the US National Institutes of Health). The performance of athletes who are stars of sports watched by millions, who may be national emblems, has enough hanging on it to become a market matter, a question of investment and expected future revenue flows from a current expenditure.

The repair aftermarket

To feed the obsession with ageing, the new frontier and new crusade of the developed countries, HRT, Omega 3 and Botox are no longer sufficient. Organ sales are on the increase and their exchanges constitute a genuine nascent sector of the economy in some undeveloped countries. With the normalization of intrusive treatments—cosmetic surgery, grafts, etc.—that used to be dramatized, this tendency indicates an evolution in the relation with the body: still essential, yes, and unique, but valued for its services, its functions, and above all its plasticity, its capacity to be adapted to improve its looks and altered to make it work better. The sale of organs does more than heal; it makes repair possible; a new part replaces a worn or damaged one. Whether by transplanting living organs or by the many sorts of prosthesis, repair technology is on the way up. And it makes improvement possible: here and there, organ purchases have been made not for survival, but for beauty or physical performance. What can one reply to the robust Israeli 60-year-old, the recipient of a kidney bought from a Hindu peasant, when he says that the graft has made the fortune of the donor's family and his own happiness? The mounting scale of this phenomenon, fed by exponential demand and middlemen who no longer bother to avoid publicity, supports the prediction that organ banks will be set up on the basis of clones or umbilical stem cells, those cells that can form any human organ, to repair existing organs or replace them.

Replacement hip joint, child's cornea, Indian peasant's kidney, cloned liver or pancreas, not to mention the ovum frozen at adolescence: the panoply available to body mechanics expands year by year. Nothing new after all: the body always renewed most of its organs by itself every ten years. Nothing new, except an acceleration of renewal. Nothing new, except that the cycle of cellular reproduction has to be obedient to will, desire and fashion. And nothing new, except the avoidance of that gradual degeneration of the cellular copies that is a major cause of physical ageing. The time is not far off when the annual check-up will include recommendations for parts that need changing, and a warning, hard to take, on the time remaining; there are still parts subject to deterioration that cannot be changed! Some are already predicting a new-style general review, to be undergone on reaching the age of seniority (probably around 60), to detect hidden faults, defective parts, and plan the treatments necessary for a long life without accidents. Such a requirement, ritualizing in its way the entry to a new stage of life, sanctioning a disengagement, at least partial, from economic and social competition, could be a way of valorizing seniority, but would be a way above all to reduce some health expenditure by detecting nascent pathologies at an early stage, and to direct more effectively certain collective investments in the struggle against ageing. More realistically, the doubling of today's life expectancy by the production and replacement of organs liable to ageing, either from cultivated umbilical stem cells (which can form any of the body's organs) or from a clone specifically intended to provide wholly compatible organs for its twin, is not so much technically impossible as politically controversial: it would confirm long life as a product, available under market conditions, with enduring well-being becoming a matter of cost. California—in secession on this matter from the rest of the US, since it authorizes the cultivation of human cells and research on replacement organs—is merely ahead of the rest in the traffic in organs and the trade in human tissue; the taboos of the human species are transgressed less by biological research than by the nascent market in human organs.

The specific orientation of this market—which has less to do with health than with the repair and transformation of the body, and is thus close to the bodily grooming, fitness or even cosmetics market, tending to become a self-image market—is apparent from the concentration of research budgets and also from some of the more sensational recent discoveries: nothing, or nearly nothing, against pandemics that affect quite significant parts of the world population; nothing, or nearly nothing, against recurrent pathologies affecting poor countries, and even less for the diseases specific to countries without social security systems; but spectacular, sometimes determining advances in anti-ageing techniques, sterility treatments and a lot of the other problems taken seriously in developed countries, some on the fringes of the healthcare area and some completely outside it.

This market is still in its earliest infancy. The price of indeterminacy, the price of freedom where the body is concerned—or the illusion of that freedom—has no limits. What does it cost to change sex? In a number of capitals in the unregulated world a body can change sex for less than a thousand euros; a man or woman can switch identities, an individual is faced with the naked will to become what he wants, or chooses, or believes ... or anyway can disappear behind the self-image that devours him.

The right of transsexual individuals—now recognized and legalized—to modify their civil status in everything but their social security number is a sometimes convulsive expression of freedom of choice. The illusion of choosing what one wants to be, the illusion of freedom where the body is concerned, in matters of sex or race, is implicit in the law that recognizes the individual's right to be what he wants, not what he is, that scrambles relations between the ego and the self ... and that in suppressing determination also does away with permanence and identity.

A market in formation

> Evian sets up a spa in the prosperous centre of Hong Kong, L'Air Liquide provides technologies for home healthcare, L'Oréal is investing in hospital cosmetics and cosmetotherapy, Danone invents the 'smiling body' to promote a curvaceous, fluid model of well-being ... the frontiers are disappearing and doctors have started talking about 'L'Oréal medicine' and worrying about their role in the emergent body industry.

The nature of the offer to provide 'healthcare' has changed with the birth of this market, with its competition and mobility. The project to eliminate all determination—of gender, race, eye colour or facial profile—is not essentially one to give care, or even to cure; it is about the production of the body, as a superior good, by way of a high value added service. Health of course, as an essential if no longer sufficient ingredient; physical fitness, well-being, attractiveness, fulfilment, happiness finally. Health, as the necessary condition for 'enjoying one's being'. So that illness has become a misdeed, an error or an accident. And so that there must necessarily be a guilty party, one who can be made to pay.

The term 'health' should be ranged with the subsidiary modalities of a demand for well-being that includes physical and moral fitness, extends into psychic fitness (what a revealing confusion arises from the words 'the smiling body', the suggestion that postures, movements and attitudes govern the emotions!) and recomposes the unity of the individual starting from the body, its flowering, its satisfaction with itself. The industry taking shape around this new product, and this new right, will bear little resemblance to the health services as we know them; for its objective is nothing less than the elimination of hazard, risk and chance. The growing assertion of a set of patients' rights, the next stage of a right to health, foreshadowing a right to well-being, are bringing increasing pressure for the industrialization of medical and hospital methods. What used to be feared, dreaded and revered in the person of the doctor is going to have to come from systems from which, by falsifying the definitions, all error will be excluded; or will have to be made good, and failing that, indemnified.

The produced, raised, full-grown body maintains, cultivates and improves itself. Above all, it protects itself. The absolute primacy of the body makes it consume anti-ageing, fitness and physical comfort services in all their aspects, from eating supposedly healthy foods to cosmetic surgery, fitness clubs, anti-depressant drugs and visits to health farms. So the debate on controlling health expenditure appears broadly to be a false debate unless it starts with this double prerequisite: can society allow its members to give free expression to their health preferences by devoting an ever-growing share of their disposable resources to them, at the cost of other services and functions that are equally important, even indispensable? What are the collective choices in terms of healthcare rights available unconditionally to all individuals, and what are the consumer healthcare choices for which society will leave responsibility, and the entire cost, to be borne by the individuals concerned? In the context of this developing awareness the question of the levels and basis of repayments seems subsidiary, almost negligible; and it means that the technical means of avoiding or reducing some serious illnesses, and of forestalling or repairing the consequences of others, instead of being kept on the sidelines, will inevitably invade the heart of the argument and bear heavily on the prospects for reducing or limiting health spending. Only health, meaning satisfaction with the self, can limit health spending; money is becoming increasingly powerless.

A stable demographic situation, a soundly established supply logic, have effects that are predictable, therefore manageable. Predictable: growth in spending on health, comfort and well-being that is consistently higher than the growth rate of GDP and inflation is written into the demography and the market of supply and demand in all the developing countries. This enables the pioneers of the new body industry to find their markets by integrating what is disconnected, by uniting what has been separated, by joining up the links in the value chain of services to the body. The preference for health spending over all other forms of consumption increases with the average age of the population, and it increases with freedom of prices, supplies and competition. It augurs an explosion in spending on well-being in the growing number of populations freeing themselves from worry about tomorrow, from the struggle for survival, and able to consume for their bodies. More than a quarter of world GDP, in ten years' time, may relate to an economic sector that is impossible to picture accurately at present, but that new coalitions of private companies and public systems, cosmetic manufacturers and care networks, agricultural and food industrialists and fitness centres, clinics or hospitals, everything from electronics and computer giants on the one hand to body-equipping centres (prostheses, subcutaneous implants for monitoring and identification) on the other, may render more legible.

A supply logic

The advent of the body and the primacy of life have this consequence: that anything and everything that can improve the body, and spare it from suffering, anxiety and ageing, will be due to it by right.

In 1960, the French spent 10 per cent of their income on clothing and 5 per cent on health. According to statistics for 2004, the French spent 10 per cent on health, spending topped up by sickness insurance, and only 5 per cent on clothing. And economists predict a steady rise in this health spending, of 1 per cent every five or ten years, under the combined effects of an ageing population, medical advances and collective enrichment. The difference is even more marked in the US where, even before the adoption of the healthcare insurance reform being promoted by President Obama, Americans were spending 19 per cent of domestic income on their health, a per capita expenditure well above that of Britain… while 40 million Americans, by choice or necessity, had no healthcare insurance at all! These figures are quite significant as they stand, but in fact they are misleading. It would be more accurate to amalgamate the health, fitness, well-being and leisure sectors, resulting in a sector representing from 20 per cent to over 30 per cent of consumption, progressing upwards alongside income, and occupying the first place in the structure of private consumption. French statistics on health spending cover only what is included under sickness insurance. The analytic session, the bottle of sleeping pills, vitamins or mood ameliorators, the surgical truss, are not counted, although they do so much for well-being; nor is the moisturizer that revives the face, or the game of golf that relieves stress. If the figures had to include all spending on health in the broad sense defined by the World Health Organization—spending 'intended to ensure lasting physical, mental and psychic well-being for the individual'—they would add to sickness insurance expenditure on medical comfort: cosmetic surgery, the costs of establishing or maintaining fitness and the spending on body and beauty care that play a part in self-image and satisfaction with the self. Expenditure—often limited to tell the truth—associated with the practice of one or more sports is naturally a part of long-term well-being, and at the same time replaces the cost of treatment or repairs. The cost of psychoanalysis, and of the legal drugs being substituted for alcohol to ensure serenity of outlook, ought to be added too. And there is a very foggy dividing line, in the minds of their consumers, between properly listed pharmaceutical products and certain new or old 'health foods', of which yoghurts claiming to act on various deficiencies or illnesses, generally without scientific proof, are the most widespread (if these cosmetics, magic creams and foods really had the virtues they claim they would be classed as pharmaceutical products and analysed, labelled and controlled accordingly, something they make every effort to avoid).

Statistics compiled in this way would attribute more than 25 per cent of expenditure by contemporary households to physical well-being, with much higher peaks in some sub-groups, notably high-income unmarried young adults and older adults having raised one or more families, but now free to enjoy a rejuvenated appetite for living. They would surely give a more accurate image of the money spent on health and the price people are willing to pay for a good life than sickness insurance figures alone. Total figures for the well-being industry are not known; but they would certainly be more meaningful than those for a sickness insurance system whose logic has been lost at the same time that its deficits were accumulating.

Those statistics are also misleading because they still refer to risk, to the chance that characterizes insurance and is so to speak its raison d'être. Insurance has lost its place in the domain of health except under rare circumstances, for the risk on which it is based is now excluded. With few exceptions, fewer and fewer indeed, medical treatment and health spending are no longer a risk that can be characterized by the probability of its occurrence; they are a certainty, reliably located in time: 80 per cent of our fellow citizens will get through 80 per cent of the medical consumption of their entire lives in their last six months. In financial terms, this justifies not insurance but fund management—management of contributions made throughout a life to finance the heavy expenses concentrated at its extreme end—falling almost entirely outside the domain of insurance, of chance and individual risk.

Where the objective used to be health, it is now physical fitness. Where the objective used to be to save from death, it is now to extend life. The theme is already present in pharmaceutical advertising, in the various messages put out by the luxury industry, the agro-food industry and the fashion industry: the well-being industry is there to extend the horizon of life, to guarantee that we will live longer while remaining attractive, in full possession of all our physical faculties, fully able to develop and enjoy ourselves. The first worldwide industry of the new millennium, the industry that is producing a new man.

Medicine in the nineteenth century precisely defined the limits of the physiological, which was what medicine addressed. The frontiers of that space are exploding outwards. In this first worldwide industry, the industry of bodies, the status of the doctor is changing, soon to be followed by that of the beauty, body-care or food industrialist. For the frontiers of the pathological, carefully established and maintained until the very end of the twentieth century, are exploding one after another. For the progressive advances of psychology and analysis have resulted in the industrial manufacture of props for the narrative and fabrication of the self. For the constitution, the recognition, the discourse of yesterday's patient have nothing in common with the discourse, the assertion, the institution of today's demander of care, comfort and enjoyment. From a responsibility to apply available means, the logic of law and rights is making the doctor responsible for achieving a result. He used to be accountable to his own conscience, his peers, the Hippocratic oath; soon he will be accountable to the market. This change is not one of demand, but of nature; the human relation, the enlightened artisanate, the risk shared by doctor and patient, are all naturally redrawn on the scales of price and value. The change of nature substitutes a mechanical industry, systems of information and codified standards, for a service centred on proximity; on complicity. Not so much giving care any more, or even providing cures, but producing. No longer a matter of first doing no harm, then seeking by all means, including listening and talking, to provide relief, but of making life a technology and the body, a product. Even, after the development some are predicting for tomorrow, of delivering the human body from birth, illness and death to enable everyone to make their bodies their finest product. There is the matter too of ensuring conformity. Such a transformation, taking medicine outside itself, almost against itself, is hustling society towards an insatiable transgression of its own limits, its own taboos, in the same implacable logic that has carried technology for the past five hundred years. Nothing is going to be too much, in the pursuit of that utopia of physical well-being, comfort and satisfaction as a right, a certainty and a due.

When the skin has a soul

> At those moments, my whole skin has a soul.
>
> Colette, *L'Éducation sentimentale*

> My best friend is my beauty salon.
>
> Sophie, aged 33

The age of indeterminacy for the body sidelines nature, origin and chance to provide the beauty, fashion and well-being industry with the unheard-of privilege of determining models of the body. The invasion of mechanisms of mass representation, photography, cinematography, then television, had the effect both of multiplying the diffusion of models to the point of obsession, and of disembodying them. Could fear of the flesh be so strong that it has forced us to fabricate those clones who parade through the women's magazines? From the effort given to banishing the very idea of ageing, fatigue and wear, a new morality is emerging, all the more powerful for being invisible, even imperceptible: an unconscious project to fabricate oneself! To extend the soul to the very surface of the skin; to choose oneself.

The cult of the body beautiful, symbolizing the sacrament of life, is celebrated everywhere with the earnest vigour that characterized ritual in the major religions; beauty is the last remaining manifestation of the sacred in societies that have abolished all the others. The result is a religion of the body, celebrated everywhere. It is to self-fabrication that the women's press, and increasingly the specialist men's press, and all the titles concerned with health/beauty/fitness/attractiveness, invite their readers; in much the same way as specialist magazines highlight the features of dream cars and motorcycles so other magazines display the muscles, postures and looks of the body, or greet the latest little black dress or skirt length, or focus on how to get him into bed on the first date, or how to shine on a girls' night out, or be the one whose swimsuit really does the trick. Because one has to believe in the body. And a new credo is really what this is about, in fitness clubs, diet sheets and Thalassotherapy centres, on analysts' couches and in personal development manuals, a credo embraced with convulsive, obsessional zeal: the credo of self-production, flanked by the demanding morality of physical beauty.

It is up to individuals to deserve their beauty. Of course, celebrating the cult called forth by this new figure of the sacred involves effort, hesitations and risks. Of course, a religion of the body finds its priests, dogmas, morality and market in indulgences. A new morality, applied in sports clubs, in dieting, by analysts, orthodontists and cosmetic surgeons, fed by leading brands, and propagated by media whose titles parade with increasing shamelessness their claim to be defining a model of life: *Young and Pretty*, *Well in My Body*, *Glamour*, *Your Beauty*. An imperative of the moral sort is what magazines covering extreme sports, appropriate thinness or liberating dietetics are projecting, a morality that changes with the seasons, capricious and mutton-headed, and all the more powerful for advancing under the double cover of freedom and number: of indeterminacy, that form of freedom turned against the self. Indeterminacy, no doubt, crossbreeding, confusion of genders, fashions and styles, but standards all the more powerful for being the passport to memberships elsewhere condemned. A new form of indulgences, acquired by a course of Thalassotherapy, a subscription to a fitness centre, a bio or vegetarian cure, the cost measuring the scale of the pardon. Not only clothes, accessories, haircut and colour, trinkets and shoes have to evolve with fashion now: the body must change too. And the age bodies have is not the one inscribed in their passports but that of the fashion projected by their musculature, skin, hair, teeth, demeanour and mimicry. Some such tendency is plain in the irresistible rise of the cosmetics industry, of the ideal of the skin as identity. It is plain in those brand slogans that since the dawn of the twenty-first century have replaced concrete promises—to erase wrinkles, tighten muscles, melt spare tyres—with the superhuman ideal of suppressing time … magic creams, pills and anti-ageing applications of this and that jostle to reassure the last generation that, no, it isn't ageing; yes, it really is rustproof, Sheffield stainless. And what used to be the product of genetics, of destiny—the blessing of beauty—ends by being listed and catalogued... For beauty spends money, even if it is not yet for sale. For it becomes an investment, the most promising there is for the thousands of girls from Venezuela, Ukraine or Ethiopia who try their luck each year in the beauty industry. For beauty is produced, and now depends on standardized canons, established and diffused with implacable authority; for beauty as self-discipline confronts all beauties of either sex with that most intractable discipline, discipline of the self.

Henceforth, the opposition between soul and body, internal reality and outward appearance, loses all meaning, since beauty is produced, since rules are there to codify, measure and protect it, since its natural insolence gives way to its reasoned production. The time of production of bodies and the time of indeterminacy culminate in the production of beauty, a beauty dissociated from all origin, culture or background, necessarily constructed even in that, but drawing freely on a repertoire of forms and codes, ethnic ones in particular, that now belong to the market and only to the market. Origin, territorial or otherwise, no longer counts. Madonna and Oprah Winfrey are leading icons of this self-fabrication that determines beauty, as choice, act of will and product; thus, as identity. For beauty gives proof of the self. For the body, the nude body, tells a story, a fuller story than analysis; it bares the soul that on the analyst's couch keeps most of its clothes on. It is no accident that naked routines, and the more difficult exercise of public undressing and dressing to which so few bodies consent easily, have become obligatory passages in modern dance; Clara Laskin, devoting a 15-minute dance piece to the undressing and dressing of several couples, staged a central image of the current reality of bodies. It is as if, with so many forms and structures discarded, the body were the last form to resist, the point of arrival and departure. Madonna, David Bowie ... today's icons are not beautiful; they have made themselves beautiful. The intensity of the labour on the self can be seen, and it makes them beautiful. Through will; through the transparent effort put into muscles, treatments, operations; and through money, which gives the hard, remodelled bodies of American, Chinese or Venezuelan women the implacable character of biometric files. Regular, white, shining teeth, hard as stainless steel; studied expression; clear, moisturized, hairless, scrubbed, deep-cleaned skin; rippling muscles; the body without a defect is an armour that annihilates nakedness by displaying nothing that fails, weakens or betrays. Anatomy may be their destiny; their own anatomy is their choice.

Metamorphosis of figures

Between 1950 and 2000, both male and female figures became taller and more slender. A Frenchwoman now is three centimetres taller and weighs 600 grams less; a Frenchman has gained five centimetres in height and lost 300 grams. This tendency is general; it is most spectacular in regions where the end of malnutrition has altered people's stature quite violently in just two generations: a Chinese man from the urbanized coast is 16 centimetres taller than his grandfather on average! Will an upward convergence turn us all into Nubas, those exceptionally tall pastoralists from the upper Nile valley who so fascinated Leni Riefenstahl?

Wealth, of course; fashion, no doubt. But above all, morality. As well as better nutrition and more consistent physical maintenance, this tendency is the fruit of an advance in self-awareness and an assumption of self-ownership that has become a moral imperative. And it is for the individual to look after his property. 'Require it of yourself'; Seneca's remark to Lucullus is appropriate today, so numerous are those who want their bodies to be a brand; the body is the individual's most visible and eminent signature, and a pitiless social marker. It is the single property that distinguishes those who money, power, origin may no longer distinguish with any certainty. Far more than the wardrobe, the body's details—predator's teeth, peachy skin waxed and plucked to the millimetre, sculpted muscles—are the image of the self. It is broadly asexual, not in its mercantile effects (despite hopes and efforts, beauty-care spending by men levels out at about 10 per cent of the total, and if moisturizing or rejuvenating creams are making some headway among them, makeup remains taboo), but overall. What does it matter if women devote to beauty what men devote to physical fitness or performance, what matter if men call it health and women call it beauty? The approach is identical, the obsession common, the tendency shared.

This trend results broadly from an accelerated cross-fertilization of fashions, techniques and signatures. The Muslim world appeared dizzily refined to Crusaders who used perfume only to drown the stench of unwashed flesh, and who did not practise hair removal; a little-known cultural import of the Crusades was the Arab lords' practice of plucking and shaving, taken up in the feudal courts of Europe. In much the same way, Yoga, meditation, tattooing and body-piercing are imports worth using to assert personality, difference, even, as it were, *not belonging*. Calling on a practice from another world means leaving the one you come from and forming your own tribe; or trying to. And it is essentially the doing of a nascent, continuously growing industry: the shaping, modification and transformation of bodies. An industry that produces mutants, but that promises more generally to enable anyone to resemble anyone they want to resemble, to make their bodies a signature, a manifesto, an assertion. Somewhere between the aestheticians who say beauty deserves itself, the biologists discovering the secrets of immortality for a large proportion of the body's cells, the geriatricians who claim that ageing is reversible given good practices and appropriate care, a new economic continent can already be seen taking shape. Some of its outlines are apparent in the reconfiguration of the distribution of mass-market products on the fringes of pharmacology and psychiatry, or in the development of consumption of all sorts of care services, fitness courses, special diets, etc. The industrialists are grabbing territory badly occupied by the liberal professions and establishing their market there: the market of the body and its moral code.

Beauty's morality

> Some of the women at Ravensbrück managed to cheat death by tinting their hair.
>
> Edgar Morin, *L'homme et la Mort*

Facing death, facing desire, the body's only support is its beauty. The place occupied by pornography in the representations, the awareness, even the art of the late twentieth century is new, in that it reveals a fascination with extreme states of the body (which transhumanism expresses in a different way). It is not there for no reason. It is the final stage of the dictatorship of desire as a driving force behind the market and growth. In some of the specialized clinics in California, Russia, Brazil or Israel, women young and not so young have their lips redrawn, fuller or finer, depending on the current models projected in men's magazines. Is this a chance to pass through the looking glass via the photographer's lens? A chance to multiply pleasure in proportion with the thousands of gazes fixed on the Playmate of the Month? One cannot help noticing that gay followed by transsexual culture, for men, and pornographic imagery, for women, have become the supreme references of physical beauty and self-image, the codes of private beauty predominating over fashion and giving beauty the exclusiveness appropriate to it ... what does it matter what everyone can see, when beauty really lies in what can only be seen by friends? And it would be interesting to examine how successive fashions in the bodies of hard-porn actors and actresses have influenced the musical scene, fashion and street style. Young adolescents, more than two thirds of whom have seen X-rated films on the internet, the TV or their parents' DVD player before the age of 14, are increasingly inclined to identify the beauty of a seductive body with the forms of porn stars of both sexes. The French rapper MC Solaar sings about Samantha Fox's imposing bosom, Madonna prances about wearing explicit soft-core S&M paraphernalia (before playing the role of a transsexual Egeria in Andy Warhol's Factory), and the lovely Elodie is one of the icons prized by teenagers. In 2002 and 2003 the flash of a G-string above low-waisted slacks was the popular expression of the increasingly strong sexual charge in beauty; it is interesting too that in renewing sexual provocativeness in the street, the school playground and the metro, it has also revived the debate on taboos and prohibitions, and rephrased the question of the public/private divide in sexuality and how open sexual play should be. More importantly though, it has expressed a new imperative that is essentially moral, covering sexual availability, provocation of desire, and the duty to be attractive.

This morality goes without saying. 'Because I'm worth it!', the L'Oréal models purr ... the body is worth everything, because nothing else is worth so much: so much time, effort, new asceticism. The spread of physical maintenance sports, sometimes to people of advanced age, is more than apparent; like the physical exercises practised by people of 70 or 80 to improve their suppleness, strength or reflexes, it can be ranged very straightforwardly alongside other health practices, but above all confirms that the body has become a material, a plastic substance that should lend itself to being changed, modelled to project the desired image. The spectacular development of piercing, tattooing, attaching jewels, rings and ornaments to the most intimate parts of the body (thus, those most worth exhibiting), corresponds to the same tendency and the same affirmation: my body is my own property, my own responsibility; I choose it, mark it, distinguish it, shape it to my will; and I can degrade, mutilate or damage it if I want. Beauty is a fabrication, all the more pitiless, demanding and costly now that the hazards of birth, conformation and the accidents of life count for so little. No one has an excuse any more for not being beautiful. Beauty as an obligation is subjacent to the discourse on beauty as a product; behind 'Because I'm worth it!' there lies a call to duty: 'because I ought to', one repeated by advertising in every possible register. Beauty is becoming a duty; the mirror carries a moral injunction.

The stern duty of the self

The promise of beauty is repeated obsessively in advertising campaigns, in brand slogans, in the springtime exhortations to put on a swimsuit; it is the promise that beauty can be produced. That it can be bought, and also that it is deserved. Behind its promise can be discerned a morality, almost an asceticism; for those who appropriate the capacity to produce themselves may seek indeterminacy, but what they get is responsibility. Parents used to give children their bodies; filiation designated primarily a process of physical reproduction, for good or ill. It is no longer the parents who produce the body; each person is responsible for his body, everyone works at modelling it, shaping it, improving its energy, its capacities and its desire, and at every moment. The habit no longer makes the monk; the body makes him, by revealing his eating and drinking habits, by showing signs of the attention or neglect given to it, by saying everything about itself, the things nothing else can say, the things that have never been said differently. And it is no longer—or no longer only—the doctor who has charge of health; the choice between good and bad conduct has to be made at every moment, in all circumstances; and at every moment one has to produce one's body, to want it to be better, to ensure its performance, its attractiveness and tone. That determination, of the skin, of the image, replaces those of filiation, culture, the social bond; it is every bit as determining and constraining as they are, every bit as dominating and exigent; even more so indeed, for the skin does not lie.

This discovery (or dizzy spell) is fuelling the rise of a new duty, the duty owed to the body. It fills the gyms, incites Danone to link movement, surroundings and nutrition in a quest for supposedly 'natural' physical harmony (the Smiling Body), suggests that the merger of Nestlé and L'Oréal (Nourishing Beauty!) could invade the field of hospital and therapeutic cosmetics. The fashion, beauty and fitness press unites with show business and magazines on sex, sport, skiing and so on to broadcast the same message: taking care of yourself, not being ashamed of your image, being able to look in the glass without quailing, are certainly major ingredients (for some) of healing, and (for everyone, throughout life) of dignity. This duty to be fit is leading to the development of unprecedented fusions, combinations, of different spheres of activity, the abrupt disappearance of divisions between hitherto separate economic fields, for example those of health and well-being. It is exposing pale sensitive skins to the sun's carcinogenic UV radiation, advancing the careers of the new gurus of 'how to eat well without having to get a bigger swimsuit', and assembling a morality. It isn't smart to be ugly. You could even say that it isn't quite the thing. Along with the individual's capacity to produce the body, his or her responsibility for it, for its attractiveness, for its performance, introduces new categories of good and bad. Everyone is responsible for his own body; and the myth of the perfect, untiring, non-corroding body conjures up another myth, that of purity, the obsession with performance, the deadly intoxication of surpassing oneself: of the superman.

The body transfigured

In this process—naturally—the body disappears. It is forbidden to be what it is—tired, dirty, wrinkled, addicted, sweaty, rumbling and panting—and required to be pure image, odourless, without moods, without excretions. The body with its blood and pus, its oozings, its blotches, its wrinkles, no longer has a place in images or words, in fact no longer has a place at all … the distaste aroused by the 'natural' odours of African or Asian crowds, in markets, buses or airports, has less to do with our habituation to an aseptic environment than with our horror of the flesh. The fascination with the body's extreme states and natural functions displayed by 'bloodbath' or pornographic cinema, and by some 'reality' TV programmes, and the existence in Europe, following Japan, of a market for unwashed underwear, are not gratuitous—they express the memory of something that no longer has an image, that has been lost in representations of the body as an exemplary value and a myth. Birth, suffering, dependency and death, in hospital or elsewhere, are vanishing from our screens, from our awareness, from representation. Long gone is the time when theologians celebrated the sweet odour of Christ's body, when prophets breathed in the scent of brave men's sweat! For the advent of the body is also its disappearance. The advent of the body is accompanied by a growing phobia for its attributes, its nature, its physiology, a terror of the body's fleshly reality ... fears assuaged by radical slimming, the fantasy of a virtual body, the dream of a body without flesh. In any case its normalization is under way. What used to be fashion in dress is becoming fashion in bodies. Soon they will all have the same teeth, the same breasts, the same lips. Armies of orthodontists, plastic surgeons and cosmetic specialists are working on it. For the advent of the body transfigures it. And many who are dead to themselves and others are not wholly reduced to a life without a self-image, without self-satisfaction, with nothing. A morality of satisfaction, frighteningly severe, is almost upon us: the body is worth keeping alive so long as it brings satisfaction to itself and others. The nude carries off the soul.[10]

An inversion is nearly complete; as a journalist in the magazine *Elle* cleverly put it, writing about a product called Happyderm: 'with this beauty cream, your skin no longer needs a shrink'. The advertising for one of those food supplements that heal without nourishing claims that 'what happens inside can be seen outside'. The soul is reaching the skin itself; indeed the soul *is* the skin, as beauty, as youth, as attractiveness. Medicine used sometimes to heal the soul to help cure the body; now the body has to be healed to ensure that the soul is all right. The cult of the self replaces all the others quite handily. It is finalizing the conditions for the advent of the body. My skin says everything about me; it is me. This determination is worth a lot of others; it threatens to become infinitely more terrible, discriminating and remorseless than all previous determinations, as if it embraced them all by transposing them into a new order, superior and unsurpassable. For to choose yourself by yourself and for yourself is the most unbearable of all choices. For the nude is offence if it is not splendour, and the struggle of the body despoiled of what flatters, what hides and distracts, is the most terrible there could be ... for nature shows through the mask, and its violence—time, fatigue, boredom, age, disgust—feeds on what represses it. For what Narcissus of either sex can fail to see the Reaper's grim stare in the mirror?

10. See in this connection Letha Cole and Mary Winkler (eds), *The Good Body: Asceticism in Contemporary Culture*, Yale University Press, 1994.

3. My Body Is My Whole Inheritance

> You can't imagine how happy it makes a man to see a woman like you. Just to look at her.
>
> Cheyenne to Claudia Cardinale in the film *Once Upon a Time in the West* (dir. Sergio Leone, 1968)

Inheritance: passed on by the forebears, due to the descendants. Among the haves, people become what they own. 'Tell me what you have, and I will know what you are', runs the timeless wisdom of peasant dynasties, and of bourgeois, industrial or mercantile tribes. Bodies submitted to it willingly; the example of the Hamburg merchants who used to marry their sons or daughters off to their Russian, Chinese or Japanese agents and representatives, has equivalents everywhere. Since the Indo-European dawn, women's bodies have been what men bought to establish lineage. From Venice to Boston, union between families through the bodies of their children underpinned the development of business (and of inheritance). Constraint through the body is a market practice.

The Code Napoléon as it applies to the family was based on this need for patrimonial accumulation and transmission in the family framework as a condition of national progress; the nuclear family, representing both closure and bond, was supposed to reproduce the function of the frontier in the political domain; by defining its space, it established a vertical link in time. The dead were less foreign than those who lived on the other side of the frontier. Our taxation system on inheritance still bears its trace, sanctioning by confiscation any transmission outside the direct parent–child line.

The history of the French over the last three centuries is first and foremost that history of bypassing the individual through transmission. It is also the history of a relation to things and to other people, the narrative of the constitution of a form by way of rituals, conventions, the private unspoken rules of families and communities … in a word the production of an *aesthetic*, that passport to eternity for discrimination. So many individuals' lives, their emotional or sexual ups and downs, their private anecdotes reduced to the commonplace, the banal, are summed up by their contribution to the estate; the only lasting thing about them that is a little bit remarkable, a bit strong, is that they have made their descendants free from want—or that they have ruined the family.

Notaries, bankers, insurance agents and other masters of inheritances have all experienced the extraordinarily powerful, even obsessive, relation of the family, of goods inherited or bequeathed, with the individual project. They have been witnesses to those moments of truth, marriages, births, deaths and divisions; divisions most of all! Reading the will always tells the same story of money, power, desire and death. The history of marriage contracts and the juridical form they impose on the association between the partners often says more about the inner lives of families than the most intimate family secrets, because goals, ambitions, resentments and regrets, preferences and rejections, emerge more clearly from them than from the routine succession of amours, betrayals and disputes. The history of inheritance law and that of contraceptive practices expose the dynastic obsession of families; suppression of the right of primogeniture explaining the two centuries of advance on everyone else achieved by French couples in the prevention of conception, and the demographic stasis between 1800 and 1940. The history of life insurance contracts (in particular acceptance of the beneficiary clause by its intended recipient, which forbids all later changes to the contract by the signatory, even when that acceptance has taken place without his knowledge) speaks volumes on human envy, interest and ambition, and reveals the unsaid: unadmitted favouritisms, shameful enrichment—black market, diversion of inheritance, family curses, incest—so that anyone who has had the chance to study the financial history of his own family emerges from the experience feeling that he has emerged from a bottomless well. The wealth of any family is an abyss unknown to the wisdom of memory.

Inheritance only came about because of the times, because there was risk and need. So that tomorrow would not be even worse; so that the future would be better; so that something of the individual would pass to his family, extending him and protecting them, accumulation was a duty and passing-on an obligation. The constraint was primarily that of survival in the relatively short term. The dreadful duty to endure, the daily chore of earning and accumulating to protect the individual and his dependants, to guard against need, against want and misery, haunted the consciousness of the French for centuries, to fade away finally at the edge of the twenty-first century. The wealth of the French is one direct outcome, and their dependence is another. Each individual was only a link in the chain of family transmission, a link supported by those above it in the chain and strained by those below it. Rather than owning the goods that were theirs, they were held captive by them from the cradle to the grave, weighed down by the commitment to maintain them. Selling or transferring was out of the question. A mortgage was a drama. 'Never sell land...'; 'If you had to sell the house...' Admonitions calculated to sound from beyond the grave, curses almost in the burden they imposed, to hold onto property, and the duty they suggested, to increase it. Inheritance is less what is received from the parents than what is owed to the children. Debt, or money owed, appears as a liability on the patrimonial balance sheet, like a loan. And no chance at all of abandoning, squandering or changing anything. Land, houses, stocks and shares, own the men who imagine they own them.

Between the members of a family, transmission of an inheritance fulfilled a function entirely different from the commonplace business of preserving wealth. It underpinned that distinction that rituals, conventions and codes build up between their adepts as a shared wealth and access to individuality. A repertoire of courtesies, precedences, formulae... It enabled the individual to choose his or her own interpretation of a given role, in a pre-existing narrative, and the faculty to construct himself using ready-made forms, by mobilizing a range of feelings, of relations, already established. As individual and family security, inheritance was an aesthetic and a morality. The assets, even on the notary's parchment, had a savour, a scent, most perfectly expressed by Mauriac's pine-forests or the overlapping Cévennes stone roof-tiles in Jean Carrière's *L'épervier de Maheux*. Who said anything about money? The family bond used to be maintained less by blood kinship and obligatory, explicit affection than by those shared sensations from beyond the narrative and even beyond memory: kitchen recipes carefully passed on, sauces and bouquet garni as rituals of belonging, housekeeping and culinary codes surviving stubbornly through the generations, gestures, postures and courtesies equivalent to passwords, a laisser-passer restoring an underlying complicity to structures behind all the words, differences and disagreements; and over it all, the mythical narrative of great moments, major ordeals of life victoriously confronted and surmounted by the ancients, statements like passports that, from cradle to grave, would ensure a place in the lineage. The obstinate liquidation of 'natural' origin and descent means liquidating a form and an aesthetic, and arouses instead the furious quest for lived experience, a quest the more furious for being beyond price: for what has to be replaced is a history, a heritage, a unique immaterial capital. And money aspires to pay for what cannot be bought, on behalf of people whose wealth it ensures while impoverishing them of themselves, in an arabesque of involuntary, copious and dramatic irony.

The horizontal society

> The number of couples changing from separate to joint ownership of property, which tripled in France between 2000 and 2005, signals a change in the order of transmission and parent–child relations (modification of the marriage contract to make the surviving partner the legatee in the event of the other's death deprives the couple's children of the share allotted to them under the former contract). Favouring one's spouse over one's children in the order of inheritance changes the relation between generations, with members of a given generation favouring each other over their descendants. It is worth recalling that in the Indo-European languages that underlie all the languages spoken on the northern shores of the Mediterranean, there were no words for husband and wife; they were designated by the words father and mother. The couple relationship was ignored by language except where it was fertile; where there was a child. Jurists who deny marriage any status other than a protective one in child-raising are referring to a millennial view that eating, drinking and sleeping together is no business of society's unless a child results. The institution of marriage has nothing to do with desire, pleasure or the couple and everything to do with the child, the transmission of the lineage and its patrimony. Far from being a couple relationship between two adults, it used to be a vertical relation, a relation with the ancestor in the graveyard, with the fathers and mothers of the spouses and with the sons and daughters to come. The man and woman were of interest to society only for their fertility ... the curse of the barren woman has always haunted the Western imagination, until the last few decades when the test tube has come to the aid of the sacred. These days, though, the couple as a contract is replacing the family as destiny. And the couple's imaginary life, romantic love, passion, is more present in public discourse than ever before, at the very moment that it is disappearing from life. A 'transformation of intimacy' (Anthony Giddens) really is taking place.

In the dark towers of their castles, in their cottages among the fields, men and women spent their lives in ceaseless dialogue with the figures of their lineages, whose words, images and stories were more immediate to them than their own lives, or those of their neighbours, in the present ... space was more distancing than time, and origin and descent registered more forcibly than contemporary reality. The presence of ancestors, living and dead, was everywhere. It contained all the figures of life and death, for the edification of the living, their penitence and submission. Tradition fixed movements and postures, and was imprinted in bodies waiting to appear. Membership of a family comprised an identity and gave self-assurance. People were closer to their dead—so often visited in the cemetery, so often mentioned in communal prayers or the family narrative—than to a living contemporary from outside the family, village or country. Every individual's personality was itself a heritage and a patrimony: the name for nobles, art for the master craftsman and journeyman, the Church fathers for the cleric, the land for the peasant. The rhetoric of blood ties rewrote the history of the Middle Ages, the Renaissance, the European revolutions, by giving everyone, his family, sometimes his country, references guaranteed to last forever; the moral comfort of nationalisms resulted. Within frontiers, generations derived from that a self-assurance that was beyond price, that of distinctness, wrongly confused today with hostility, discrimination or closure. Behind the historically manipulated assertion of a reconstituted purity (cheapening the mixture of Indo-European peoples from which the European nations emerged) lay the solid reality of families and their land and a genuine patrimonial plan, the key to progress: that everyone felt bound to their relations through the transmission of family holdings. A man was a man because he came from *here*—from a place—and from *them*, from a lineage; John Paul II meant nothing different when he said that every man belongs to humanity through his nation. That belonging, whether embraced or resisted, enables the individual to show passion and certainty at difficult moments. A service from the memory, guarantor of confidence, that is worth as much as others.

Business, via the white-collar classes, was the essential instrument of a new relation between men, horizontal this time; the economic relation, the relation with society through labour, sanctioned by money. Money disconnects people from time, distances them from the land and their relations, and puts them in touch with others through the market. In a century, more than half the French population has been brought by business and industry into towns, factories and the wage economy; this transformation, now complete, with less than 10 per cent of the population genuinely independent (whose income is neither a salary nor the product of a commercial agreement disguising a subordinate economic relationship), has marked human life far more deeply than the accompanying political changes, although it is true that some of these have also played a part. Over the past three decades, businesses have wrought an accelerated change in the nature of French and European populations, by establishing a vast market in bodies between the continents. For the main business of life, which used to be to reproduce oneself and perpetuate the species, is no more. For the priority of the family—being and having, the kinship bond, discovery and transmission of the self—has given place to the priority of work. And the main business of earning a living, now that the land no longer ensures an arduous but certain living to everyone, has displaced the anxiety to preserve and pass on.

We need to measure the consequences of the liberation achieved by the market economy and money: the waged and salaried classes. They made the myth of urban America, and that novel power unique to the twentieth century, a power based on industry. In a single century 20 million Frenchmen left the land, the workshop, the small business, to join the staff of an enterprise, abandoning the world of their forefathers, of tradition, to enter the world of production. Enterprise cut across villages, classes, families, to make a society from all of them. Through the rhythms of work, the sharing of skills and techniques, it brought together those who had been separated by their origins, their land, sometimes their language and their religion. They had been heirs, even perhaps above all when their heritage was only a name or a tradition; they became comrades. The factory taught them what the elders would pass on no longer. Analysts of business as an economic form are blind to the first function it fulfilled, a function of social transformation: ensuring the passage from land to wages, bending men to shiftwork, timetables, shared labour, processes; constituting men as a generation and no longer as a lineage. The industrial entity that resulted is beautifully conveyed in Chaplin's *Modern Times*. Industrial enterprise was the effective link in the transfer of a majority of the population from the country to the towns. With the transfer complete, with more than two thirds of humanity living in or close to towns, this link will lose its function. Is there any guarantee that enterprise will survive?

After the Industrial Revolution, despite the reservations of traditionalists and the Catholic church—in those days more suspicious than socialists of the technological society and big industry, and doubtless more clear-sighted too—business and industry became the passing place for the individual in the group: the seat of social manufacture, where each individual's output measured his usefulness to his fellows; a setting, too, where everyone could assert himself through a class bond, the certainty of virtue, impatience for the future and the warmth of the group. A sort of idealism, by turns grandiloquent and moving, and politically ambiguous, expressed this leading function of industrial labour: placing everyone in the service of the collective effort, whether the objective was national, the furtherance of class struggle or the promotion of a better future. The work may have been anonymous, fragmented, broken down, but nevertheless acquired a nobility that earlier times had denied it, by being the link between self and self; founding a community by forging an identity for those who, having lost the land, would never again play the role assigned by tradition.

But this bond is unravelling too. The growth of financial rights in inheritances and incomes on the one hand, and the increase in assistance incomes on the other, are marginalizing labour in the formation of net income over a lifetime. CNN, financial markets, new laws, the ideology of universal rights, have made us resemble Chinese, Russians or Brazilians more closely than our own grandparents. Horizontal solidarity between members of the same generation, proclaimed, cultivated and enforced through public levies, demolishes the vertical solidarity that unites the different generations of the same lineage, down through the cycles of life and death. An intense process of liquidation of blood ties, which used to underpin common law, common custom and inheritance, is under way; and it appears a positive opening to those who do not see the more subtle and violent separation of the world that it forebodes. The wellspring of universal representations spouts like a geyser to diffuse a new moral order, making each of us the friend of all the world and our own enemy. It means to spread a soft, common identity to which no one can claim to be foreign, for no one can escape its motor: the market. An open society wants to give history the sack and define itself by relations between contemporaries alone, forgetful of what is coming, and where it is coming from. To liberate oneself from heritage and memory is a way to find oneself; it is also a way to forget time, to avoid growing old (or to think so), and to forget how to die.

The last generation

> In gaining long life, Europe and Japan have lost eternity. This earthly life which used to be a passage, an ordeal, a grubby image of that other, real, eternal life, has become all of life and all there is to life. We have gained long life by losing eternity, make no mistake. We even have to work to free ourselves of the last vestiges of superstition, dizziness, pre-digested thought, that might suggest something coming after us would count in any way. We even have to eliminate those lies to the effect that the world does not end when we do. A whole generation, our generation, is devoting itself to those ends with application and efficiency. It is the first to take in the meaning of the disappearance of the sacred, the running-down of history and the loss of eternity; it is the last generation. For what could follow it, what could count for it, a generation that no longer expects salvation except for its body?

Europe (along with Japan) differs sharply from all other regions of the world in this respect: death is no longer doing its job there. The renewal of generations is no longer occurring there because the old people are not leaving the space for it. They are occupying it themselves. If it were not for donations—fortunately stimulated in France by the reduction in inheritance tax, and also by the many displays of internal solidarity by the members of families (more than 20 billion euros are transferred each year between elders and their descendants, mainly outside the tax system and strict inheritance law)—the concentration of property in the hands of the oldest would be made explosive by the combined effects of positive real interest rates and lengthening lifespans; people in their sixties who have had to run their professional and family lives without the help of any inheritance would be inheriting from near-centenarians turned into euro millionaires not by work, but by time. People who have retired young inheriting from old retired parents: that is already the situation of a majority of French families, people not inheriting from their parents until they have themselves retired. The concentration of social benefits—from a system whose deficit is already approaching 10 per cent of GDP—on the retired population (non-payment of social security contributions, various tax rebates and allowances, subsidized transport and entertainment, privileged access to leisure facilities, etc.) will sooner or later become unaffordable, an accumulation of privileges that puts social expenditure in the place that used to be occupied by inflation, but with the opposite effect on redistribution; it helps pensioners in substantial credit instead of young active adults in debt.

The generation that counts, that earns and votes, the one that walked straight into jobs during the postwar golden age, that fought to leave the family home at 18 for a garret (but with a view), the one that conquered co-education, that made May '68 and voted Doors, Beach Boys or Deep Purple, has been the vector for the advent of the body. It has brought it about without wanting to, or even being aware of it. This is not a lost generation or a sacrificed one. It is the last. It is not going to give up its place in a hurry. It means to endure and to profit thereby. It refers glibly to the end of history and dreams of an everlasting present. It is breaking away from the historic orientation of liberalism, which aspired to progress and was firmly bolted to the naïve project of ensuring a better life for future generations. Who still believes in that? And it is the last because it wants to be perfect: because the morality of self-production, which teaches that no one depends any longer on anything but their own will and their own choices, excludes want, error and death. It dreams that the world stops with it, claims a monopoly of good for its own advantage, and intends to exploit the world and its rights in good conscience. In its indifference to reproducing itself and passing on, in its casual dismissal of history and the world, the perfect generation trumpets its refusal to supplement itself through others, to ensure a lineage to fill a lack it does not feel, and to disappear that something better might come. Political leaders used to promise to change the world. Now they will be elected because they assure us that the world will not change *us*; that time and history have forgotten this generation, and all the resources of the economy will be devoted to ensuring its safety, well-being and self-satisfaction.

Consent to the ever-increasing public deficit resulting from expenditure on consumption and not investment, like the accelerated destruction of natural resources—the liquidation of the conditions on which human existence and economy were based[1]—signals a shift in awareness and a change in collective preferences. For the first time, the word 'progress' is not applied to future generations, is not part of the transmission process, but designates what I can do for myself to make life better now. And for the first time, we will not only have failed to extend the farm and pay off the debts, we will have sold the land and passed on some debts. It is not impossible that those who attribute the collective malaise to the breakdown of social mobility are mistaken. Indifference to the future is the root

1. See Hervé Juvin, *Produire le monde—pour une croissance écologique*, Gallimard, 2008.

of the problem and does not eliminate fear of history. Withdrawal into the present and into the self blunts perception. A foggy mixture of anxiety over the environment, fear of science and a feeling of helpless inability to act generates a reluctance to pass anything on. It is less a matter of selling the future to the present than of suppressing it altogether. Solidarity between the generations and national solidarity have become the pretexts for the calculated selfishness of the baby boom generation. Where transmission is concerned, the state is riding roughshod over the duty to accumulate by writing blank cheques on the account of future generations to finance the comfort of retired people and the very old, when its job really is to finance young people to start their lives, or promise them a life proportional to their contribution. And as for preparing for the future, the abandonment of all plans and the loss of the ability to act by the public authorities are revealing enough. Individuals and families are going to have to cope with a future that the state seems determined to ignore.

From that indifference to the deficits of public systems—which are digging an abyss of debt under the feet of future generations, and will drastically reduce their capacity to act and freedom of choice, to the point of total inaction on the environment and management of scarce resources—signs pointing in this direction are multiplying. Perhaps the most telling is that, on the matter of collective anxiety over the future, in Europe and the US the worry of parents still at work over their own retirement situation has overtaken their fears for their children's job prospects.[2] Yet those children are really going to need jobs, and well paid ones, to pay back all the borrowed money that has been lavished on their parents.

Working for eternity

Every species seeks to perpetuate itself. It fulfils that purpose through reproduction; no sexed species cares very much what happens to individuals when they are too old to reproduce. But we have stopped being like that. Not only because reproduction can happen differently, but because immortality for the individual ensures perpetuation of the species without reproduction or transmission. Our secret, buried dream is of a time that no longer passes, leaving the institutions of heritage and transmission lying neglected, like fishing boats on the shores of devastated oceans. An organism that renounces reproduction can gain eternity. For the

2. Study conducted by Axa, USA, in May 2004.

> immortality of the individual is as good as sexed reproduction, since both ensure survival for the species. The Buddhist concept of ahimsa is becoming a central figure of our time: the transcendence of all desires not through abstinence, but through fulfilment.

Human beings are not made to die. In every living species, there is a close relationship between ageing and reproduction. A large part of an individual's biological capital is used up in reproducing. In the decision not to reproduce, or to reproduce parsimoniously, there may be an indication of a preference for prolonging life, with the escape clause that a generation that was going to live forever would not need to reproduce. Transmission would be unknown to it, because it would be pointless. The major break now taking place concerns the relation between length of lifespan and the moment when reproduction occurs, and also between lifespan and the number of children. Until quite recently the number of children was only limited by the woman's childbearing capacity or the death of one of the spouses. This is no longer the case. It is also interesting to note that the right of primogeniture favoured large families, since the question of dividing up the land, business or other property did not arise; fear of having to divide or dismember estates is what lay behind the first French contraceptive practices.

We have not reached the end of the life-expectancy adventure with its dream of immortality, and its reality of a white-haired society.[3] Contrary to what common sense suggests, the probability of dying does not increase with age. Neurobiologists and gerontologists are discovering an unexpected situation. The estimated ceiling of around 110, the maximum age to which those who are not lucky mutants might expect to live, has risen. We now have some early statistical data on very old people, aged over 100. And the data suggest we need to look further still. It is false to regard death as characteristic of life. On the contrary, the character of life is to endure. Primarily through reproduction, but also through its own refabrication, its own cellular reproduction, even without going so far as downloading the individual's whole intelligence, memory and sensibility into a computer, making it possible to transfer him or her into a new body any number of times (as promised by the militants of transhumanism). The difference is that to prolong life resulting from sexed reproduction

3. See Pierre-Henri Tavoillot and Eric Deschavanne, *Philosophie des âges de la vie*, Grasset, 2007, which explores the increasingly problematic character of maturity.

involves individual death, and calls another male or female individual to life, while to prolong life by improving its biological programming and correcting anomalies, flaws or pathologies, does not involve death and excludes the other. An individual's son or daughter is at once closest and most foreign to them, for it is through our children that we die: we die that they may live. We do not know what the intoxication of 'the last generation' can produce. But we are already there.

Getting there, at least. Part of today's 55–75 age group in Europe lives, behaves and manages itself as if no generation should follow it. Through its votes, and even more through its wealth, it holds an effective political majority (in the 2005 British elections the proportion of eligible voters whose vote was determined primarily by pension levels was 34 per cent; more of these voted than members of other categories, giving them about 40 per cent of the votes cast; so in effect, no one can be elected in old Europe against the wishes of retired people, or indeed without their support). It is enjoying the peace dividend and the mastery, the *ownership*, of a world that still seems to be offered to it on a plate, from Bali to Florida and Shanghai to Cape Town. And it thinks all of that is its well-deserved due. For is that not the message that has been addressed to it at such indulgent length, over four decades of steadily inflating rights? The unstemmed gushing of the discourse on rights has done just as much as the break with tradition to help divert solidarity. In its economic and social choices, through manifestations of solidarity that could be called exclusively horizontal—between members of the same generation, with others excluded—this generation shows itself forgetful of its debt to its predecessors and neglectful of those to come, who will have not only to pay its debts but also to live with the effects of its frenzied demolition of European structural capital. Hampered from the start by this moral conundrum: it is death that makes life, and how can people live, how can they grow up, how can they be themselves, when their parents refuse to die, when the space is still occupied, when the time for mourning never comes?

The preference of a conserving society for the indefinite prolongation of individual survival is established in France; the scale of public spending, supposedly on social security or 'support', approved to this end (retirement homes, dependency benefits, geriatric services, home care, etc.) is the overpowering expression of a tacit choice. Never has a society devoted such means to ensure the survival of individuals incapable of reproducing, to rejoice in their sterile conservation against their dignity and against their will, until the point has been reached that in some parts of the country, the only prospect of employment for the young is to serve the aged, as 'living companions' in their dwellings or at the retirement home. Never has a society spent so lavishly, not on health, but on an obese and illogical system of conservation. Only the vertigo of eternity can explain an unadmitted, unspoken—unconscious perhaps—consensus on the cost of prolonging the lives of very old people and casualties of living. The consequences of what is certainly a reordering of public expenditure are never clearly stated. Hemiplegics, sufferers from Parkinsonism and others are granted during the last months or years of their lives, without the slightest benefit in terms of quality of life or self-realization, tens of thousands of euros by a society that in many cases had not given them a fraction of that during their active lives. This consensus that dare not speak its name concerns a massive redistribution under the pretext of indirect salary from the active young to their elders and above all to the health system itself.

We need to draw the lesson of the disastrous swerve that occurred between 1970 and 1980 in the distribution of funds, when the public retirement systems chose to yield to the immediate demands of pensioners (by awarding free grants, by lowering the level of contributions, by supplementing patchy careers free of charge) rather than organizing the future of those working and still paying contributions. Such public policies express a wish to stop time and do away with history. Not a willingness to immerse ourselves in a common undertaking that will only end with the species, but a determination that the species must end with us. Political transcendence is sidelined by the revolution of perfect bodies. Our perfection ought to make us immortal. With tradition already liquidated, we have only to liquidate the future to enjoy in peaceful solitude our perfect selves, and their rights. This is not just a matter of stopping the unfolding of history as change, power struggle, ownership conflict, contract breakage, resetting debts and credits at zero, but of ending everything—belief, ideal, Nation, origin—that might enable others, our children, to perceive themselves as historical subjects, able to make history, to dishonour their debts and tear up their IOUs. Education, current received thought and the ideology of the market are all working at it with extreme tenacity. The new morality is limited to money and contracts passed between individuals; in the transformation of intimacy as analyzed by Anthony Giddens, relationships between consenting adults, of which marriage remains the widespread form, ought to ensure fulfilment for everyone, through the constant renegotiation of the compromise between individual interests that enabled them to form in the first place. The same applies between the generations; the contractual mode becomes the object of all behavioural morality. Payment discharges all debts: couple, child, undertaking, promise, passion ... there exists no contract that cannot be reduced to a matter of price. The religion of the contract ought to ensure eternity for a perfect world, one without history, without oblivion, without distance and without forgiveness.

> Like the Inuit who call themselves Unuoyagut—the real human beings—relegating the American Indians who had driven them from the forests to the status of lice, Iqkrelek, we are always ready to think that humanity is what we have become, and that we are the model for what will follow. This sentiment masks another, the idea of the birth of the superior man. This generation is behaving as if it were the last. But our idols are sterile. As usual, big words—solidarity, respect, attention—have disguised attitudes that are exactly the opposite; solidarity with contemporaries, to buy peace and tranquillity; gross indifference to those who will follow us, who will bear the debts contracted in their name.

Broken bond

> Through the lying use of words, housing estates abandoned by God, where the sun never shines, from which the good earth cannot be seen, where friendship (which Heidegger believed essential to life) is non-existent, are dignified with the name—but only the name—of city.[4] Perhaps this collective lie is what provokes the individual derision of the nicknames adopted by graffitists, rappers, taggers and break-dancers: to bear a name is to accept the law of heritage and of transmission. But how can one accept a name when society uses words dishonestly?

Human societies used to define themselves, as they still do for the most part, by bonds of descent, by vertical links—which have made all experienced, red-blooded, active societies think of themselves essentially in historical terms, through their own history. Vertical links to heroic narratives encouraging pride in the self (the first objective of primary education being to inculcate this pride in one's origins, which ensures a collective identity and enables everyone to be integrated into a common outlook,

4. Translator's note: Housing estates are referred to in France by the word 'cité'.

forming the basis of solidarity); links between forebears and descendants, governing memberships and connections, binding communities together through absolute successes or exemplary misfortunes, always shared; links repudiated by the society of the body and isolation. These bonds are being erased. The ties of parenthood, too determining to be acceptable, were the object of radical subversion over two decades between the 1970s and the 1990s. Children born in the 1970s and 1980s are no one's children, for their parents refused, with great energy and greater perversity, to perform their role. Rejecting the determining one of parenthood to be the pals, friends or accomplices of their children, since they could hardly become their lovers. These same defaulting parents now seek their children's advice on what to wear, where to go and how to throw a party, and these same children are now having to reason with parents so liberated that their lives are without direction. Bonds of origin and descent, of religion or faith, of the land and shared history, have lost their legitimacy, when they have not become too controversial to mention ... it goes without saying these days that no one works or invests for their own families, only for humanity. Internet, satellite TV and the mobile phone are some of the tools that make it possible to be somewhere without being there, to frequent unknown strangers and inhabit a territory without belonging to it, establishing the conditions for an intense way of being, present to everyone, everywhere and nowhere; and excluding any wish or sentiment of participation, of being a responsible link in a chain.

The implicit choices in Europe—non-reproduction of the original population, indifference to the living conditions of future generations, multiplication of empty commitments to pay later—proceed from the emergent belief that humans do not have to die. They apply rigorously that principle that lies behind 'the sufferings of the young thirty-year-old':[5] all that counts is what counts to me. Disengagement from all ties is a value. A market value that pays, in the human market now taking shape in a multiplicity of exchanges invisible to our formatted, shuttered gaze.

Mobility, fluidity, reversibility: those technical and systemic objectives have taken us over. They have become our nature. Like downhill skiers, surfboarders skipping crosswind at improbable speeds, crouching surfers swooping down the pipe, the life models held out to all of us as examples are models of gliding, as different as they could be from the ones called

5. Marya Goyet, *Les souffrances de jeune trentenaire*, Albin Michel, 2005.

taking root, duration, depth. Cleared of all frictions, roughnesses and snags. Freed from commitments, delays, feelings, from everything that holds back, slows down, catches. Detached. And universal, without frontiers, without connections, without territory. Thoughtless too, refined, unashamedly out of touch with reality. Without rules, limits or structures. Without anything dependent on the self, that attaches or weighs down. Memory is in the USB port, links are internet links, community is the web. The journey is the route, not the destination. Liquidity becomes a supreme value, the absolute expression of rootlessness, the stuff of extreme wealth as of extreme destitution: for on the heels of liquidity there always comes liquidation. And speed is a value, rhythm an ideal, whatever the music, whatever the horizon.[6] Until such time as different bonds and new territories form out of the break, disconnection remains a current figure. It constructs isolation, it facilitates the formatting of opinions and of expression. Can that be called freedom?

Work in progress

> 'Completing something takes nerves of steel', Delacroix said. No doubt; we no longer bother to do it. More and more artists are refusing to allow the words 'The end' to sign off their work; apart from that, they are reluctant to leave any practice, attitude or emotion to fade in a 'work'. This refusal is premonitory. For it is reality, facts, time, that we deny will ever arrive. That something should have happened, that it should be irremediable, finished: that is what is becoming intolerable. Reality is intolerable. And digital techniques have appeared, with unexpected strength, to make it possible for nothing to happen that cannot be corrected, reviewed, changed; to enable nothing to be completed that might turn out not to be what we wanted it to be.

Unexpectedly, invisibly, the technical revolution introduced by digital, wireless and soon biological technologies has been as staggering in its effects as in its discretion. The computer memory, the network, the microchip are moving on from the status of tools to facilitate, amplify or automate, to the status of functions to supplement or extend the functions of the human individual. In the process they free up energies, inclinations and capacities. Think in terms of a sensory universe in which the virtual and the real interpenetrate and become entangled, a mental

6. See Peter Sloterdijk's essential *La mobilité infinie*, Seuil, 2002.

universe in which the rational and the irrational are no longer separate; try to imagine collective worlds in which common intensity, rhythm and sensation make the society that is no longer made by institutions, projects, faith or the enemy.

We need to imagine this because we are gradually departing from the oneness of human life, caught in that space-time where the body lies. Digital techniques are at the origin of a transformation of reality. Silver iodide photography, based on a cluster of optical, mechanical and chemical processes, froze a still image of the world, while the movie camera froze a succession of such images tracing a movement of the world. That determination of reality and time is all over now. Digital cameras capture sequences of information on the world—colours, faces, expressions, movements—but only to deliver them as raw material to the user, who has instant access to a capacity hitherto only available to God: to make what he or she wants of that material. History is not what has occurred, but what is represented as having occurred; the truth is not in the moment when the shutter opens, it is whatever its author wants to make of it.

This invention of a liquid, fluid, reversible reality should be seen for what it is: a new break, in which the oneness of reality, the solidity of facts, proofs, statements, the dependability of the past, are disappearing. Using the first avatars of a living actor's body to play a number of very different characters, the film *The Polar Express* (dir. Robert Zemeckis, 2004) marks a new level of indeterminacy, one that could enable deceased actors to play in new films, that could make it possible for historically important individuals to replay, in their old age, episodes from their youth. It puts the filmmaker in the position of a novelist or composer of musical pieces: in absolute control of the medium and material. It transforms the economic value of a star by disconnecting his or her image from physical ageing: a virtual avatar will never grow older. Biometrics and animation techniques, applied to an actor or actress, will enable the filmmaker to adapt the digital recording of a virtual character to play anything, at any time, at any age; the cinematic clone already exists and promises to transform the respective functions of director, actor and scriptwriter. It would be possible today to shoot—or rather, make—a feature film starring a 30-year-old Marilyn Monroe; and just as possible to make her play Greta Garbo's mother or Isabelle Adjani's sister. With historic figures the possibilities are even more dizzying: imagine a repentant Hitler in front of the Wailing Wall, Stalin praying at the entrance to the Gulag, Geronimo and

Theodore Roosevelt signing a treaty ceding New Mexico to the Sioux people…

The conditions of transmission, which used to be based on an identity through time, are being transformed. Because although only a little of the texture of life is being lost, a good deal of the oneness of life and of the individual is going with it. It is no longer just a matter of maintaining a perpetual present, but of ensuring that nothing really happens. Various things—the seasons, nature really—were once expected to represent the immutable passage of time and teach wisdom in the face of death, acceptance of ageing and its renunciations. The reality of a digital world says the opposite: that time, old age and death are only what separate us from the other world, the world of the screen: our world. Space and time used to dictate to the body by defining its reality, its specific reality and that of its surroundings. We are starting to reverse that relation, in the first place by producing the body, and after that, nowadays, by replacing the physical environment with a virtual one where all codes, all standards of evidence, all so-called laws of 'nature', can be falsified, hijacked or rendered meaningless. The fascination with the term 'relativity' coined a century ago by Einstein has spread as the relativity of time and space, and of our experiences, the appearances of the world and our received certainties, has become more apparent, and as technology—of memory, of the screen, of information—has begun to invade, to supplement and *improve* reality, or replace it with a world governed by the body. The true advent of the body is here, in this subjection of time, space and the real to its demands, its rhythms and emotions, its satisfaction. A different 'end of history' can be discerned in the capacity to produce an emotional and sensory environment, immutable in its essential components and continuously renewed in the way these components are combined and arranged, another way of ensuring immortality for a generation that has found the means to fill up screens, stage and imagination, beyond itself, its talent or projects, through the brilliance of a technology able to promise that generation that, for it, the bell will never toll. 'That must never be allowed to happen again!' has become 'nothing must ever happen again' … let nothing more come out of history that is really historical. But the last generation has not weighed properly the meaning of its rejection of history, time and death. Openness about death makes it possible for every individual to take his place in the succession of generations. A generation that will not die is preventing its children from taking their place in the chain of life and condemning them to watch passively as history continues elsewhere, without them.

Long lifespan as a material asset

When we are so close to realizing the hope of making every individual responsible for the good management of a lifespan that, for many, will exceed a hundred years, the meaning of death changes: it is no longer an ever-present risk, and the sky is no longer threatening. Life, the time of a long life, becomes an asset; even, for those who have everything, the only asset that counts. Quantity of life, measured statistically in the mortality tables as remaining life expectancy at any given age, enables a figure to be set on what is meant by a good life, something no longer measurable in quality or aesthetic terms. It is no longer true that we do not know the day or the hour; we can situate them in an improbable, remote later, their menace weakened, their grumblings diluted, lost in the tumult of the everyday. Others may place them in a near future and try to come to terms with them; there is a growing market in extreme old age support, education for dying.

That century of life, that right to a century of life, clears the stage of the remains of the divine so that we can occupy it newly remade, under our own colours and dancing to our own tune. Nature and the gods had linked roles. Thunderbolts, wild beasts, plague, famine, accident, snatched back the lives grudgingly conceded to people reminded daily—by terror of the heavens, among the pillars of the temple, from behind the sorcerer's mask—of their condition as survivors on sufferance. That conceded life is now an owned life, an asset; anyway, a flourishing industry is working hard to tell us so and make us believe it, the better to sell us the means to that life. Health and well-being magazines and TV channels help us to make the right choices, to devote the bulk of our leisure time to 'looking after ourselves': maintaining our health, improving our diet, abolishing stress, formatting our bodies to secure that fund of life that is our due.

Much more, surely, than the lengthening of lifespan in itself, this phenomenon of the appropriation of long life represents a revolution in the human condition. In 1900, as in 1000, with some variation between decades or centuries, men and women died at any age. In those times there was no guarantee that a child who had survived the weeks and months of peak infant mortality would not be hit at 20 or 40 by a deadly infectious disease, die of tetanus at 30 or 50, succumb at 40 or 60 to the heart attack brought on by poor diet and exhausting labour, or indeed become one of the rare and venerated very old people in their eighties apparently forgotten by time, gazing distantly on a motionless world from which all their close contemporaries had departed.

It is probable that in 2010, 80 per cent of an age group will reach the threshold of their biological life expectancy, today over 85 for men, over 92 for women. This will result in part from the withdrawal of social approval from behaviour risky to the self and others—smoking, drinking, dangerous driving—but in larger part from the detection during childhood and early treatment of grave but inconspicuous pathologies. The impassioned quest for cures, the new pursuit of physical fitness and time-defying youthfulness, the quest—illusory for how much longer?—for choice of age, have already had this consequence: people hardly ever die young these days, in our wisdom-crippled West, unless by conscious or unconscious choice, increasingly conscious and soon entirely so—tobacco, alcohol, careless driving, risky sexual practices are among the things that cause early deaths that bodily chance now only causes in exceptional cases—or by genetic curse, notably deaths from childhood and young adult cancers.

What is new is that we claim to be the owners of this lifetime. We have legal rights over our lives. My life is my own property; it is the only one of its kind; and because of its uniqueness, it is the only one that will do. What is new is that an intolerance of risk, mistakes, any incident that may harm that asset is growing, and with it a suspicion of all those—the pharmaceutical industry, doctors, surgeons, radiologists, anaesthetists—whose products or interventions are the guarantors of those rights. The law is gatecrashing the operating theatre, pinning the contract to the bedhead. A formalized right to an outcome is not far off; the questioning of professional medical responsibility in civil law, laws protecting the disabled, compensation for victims of environmental illnesses, the obsession with eliminating discrimination of all sorts, all point that way. A new territory of the law is being born, appearing gradually over the last 20 years in a court verdict here, a judgement there, apparently disconnected but coherent over time in the elaboration of life as an asset. The fraught subject of hospital-caught infections and compensation for their victims (outnumbering road accident victims nearly two to one in France); the judiciarization of medicine, increasing its costs to a point where professional responsibility among certain exposed categories—surgeons, anaesthetists, obstetricians, radiologists, immunologists, cardiologists—has become uninsurable, making medical tourism more attractive. Behind the right to be spared suffering, the right to die with dignity, if necessary to benefit from an assisted death, the declared right to dietary, medical and public security, understood to mean a zero-risk requirement, a new social demand is taking shape: for the peaceful and secure enjoyment of the lifespan that medicine promises.

While political and social effects are not absent, the most certain effect of the long life promised to the majority will be patrimonial; the lifetime becomes an asset. This space of a long lifetime that I inhabit, where I live, is mine. It is my property. And evil to him who tries to touch it; to take what is mine. For this patrimony is unique; all other elements tend to be related to it, to have meaning only through and for it. It is a different advent of the body, a patrimonial and juridical advent. Other elements of an inheritance are only worth what they contribute to the asset of long life. Those who possess a body promised long life and capable of good-living no longer own themselves; they belong to that body, to that good-living, as a duty, an obligation, a constraint almost. The duty of medicine is not just to cure; it has the obligation to guarantee the entire lifespan as given in the mortality tables, which belongs to me: anyone daring to restrict it is stealing my property. The body is managed like a property, now being spent, now saved. The law, the bank, the market, will not be slow to lay hands on this new relation to time, duration and the self. We should get ready for politicians whose main direction and primary assessment criterion will boil down to their public health policy, their well-being and environmental quality policies ... policies for the body whose essential objective is to enjoy the patrimony of long life.

From one patrimony to another

I have only this body; I *am* only this body; with its death I will lose everything... Transforming the body into an asset, and a sole asset, abolishes some of the historical origins of transmission and some of the psychic reasons for it, while overturning millennial speculations on heredity.

Leading sports stars were the first to understand this. Their athletes' bodies were the capital on which interest payments—in the form of starting money or match fees, fees for advertising appearances, etc.—could ensure a high standard of living. An asset that had to be taken care of from the start, constantly maintained and (if possible) improved. An asset to be managed over time, to be spared from risk, strain and excesses. An asset to be kept going, by providing it with the best possible conditions for stability, expression and fulfilment.

Today there are millions of people—go-ahead youngsters, lawyers, managers, commercial and civil service executives—who know that their physical capital is their main asset in life; their only asset. They are in the body market. They know that, contrary to the stifling rhetoric of equality, the beauty, grace or attractiveness of the body is becoming a selection criterion, a pitiless social marker, and the last remaining link to reality: those directors of human resources who make participation in high-level sport a determining factor when hiring staff know that bodily discipline is replacing the lost disciplines of mind and character. The only distinguishing factor, now that academic competition is so distorted, now that all membership, connection, is denied, is the body: the control, the posture, the tone of the body say of any man or woman what their pedigree no longer says. Masters of the body—masseurs, dieticians, beauticians, plastic surgeons—are acquiring a hitherto unnoticed authority. The athletics, swimming or judo trainer now has the authority that the teacher abandoned, most notably when schools stopped keeping the body in line—stand straight, head up, shoulders back, sit down, stand up, don't tip your chair back—that rough and ready bossing that used to train the group. And people who cannot sit still in school, because no one has ever made them do it, report with a correct, formal bow on the mat because the master requires it. And people who go to school if they feel like it, and behave badly when they are there, willingly submit in the evening to the ingenious tortures dreamed up by sprint trainers for their pupils on the athletics tracks around Paris.

Evita, from Ukraine, who passed out in the Metro as a result of starving herself to look better for her first modelling jobs; Joseph, from Cameroon, who became Carl Smith's pupil, took a diploma in finance at the University of Miami on the strength of his weight-lifting and broke the 10.1 seconds barrier for the 100-metre sprint; even Lina who became one of Edinburgh's most sought-after escort girls through strength of will, fasting and practising the complicated postures required for Scottish love-making: all understood that their bodies are the main tool of their trade, and not only because they are bodies for sale. They are experiencing the new freedom of the market in bodies, in relationship, in performance, a change that has led many liberal thinkers into favouring the liberalization (and 'professionalization') of prostitution, sex-change operations paid for by health insurance, medical help with voluntary death and legalized doping (under medical supervision) in sport. They are a generation ahead. But white-collar workers are starting to understand something they have known for a long time without admitting it to themselves: the body is an essential asset. Managers, businessmen, are discovering that their physical appearance is related to their performance. Women, and some men these days, know that their skin is their asset, and will influence their lives. They are faced with a world where the body says more than any amount of wardrobe, where its freedom, ease and agility almost make clothing superfluous: where the body is the most important social marker. They inhabit a world where respect for physical integrity, and even perhaps the satisfaction of all physical desires, are erasing moral notions often accidental in origin, unstable in application, and sometimes so tragically distorted. In their working lives, leisure pursuits and lifestyles, they take account of a disturbing reality: success at school and university, in professional and public life, is closely linked to physical beauty. The gap exists at every stage of life: children considered 'beautiful' by their peers and by adults are 40 per cent more likely to complete their education without dropping out; young adults considered 'good-looking' by their work colleagues and professional circle are 40 per cent more likely to have regular promotion and an upward career path, without periods of unemployment; they are also better placed to meet the beautiful woman or handsome man whose partnership will help them in life, etc. The same gap can be found in retirement homes, where tenants thought 'attractive' by their neighbours, meaning in this case without disabilities and not demented, are the most likely to live longer, without health crises or behaviour problems. And the importance of this gap is increasing as other criteria of preference fall into neglect or contempt, with the steady loss of what used to be called civilization, which clothed bodies in politeness, among other attitudes and rituals.

Transmission broken down?

> My two boys have learned to love what is beautiful. A good wine, a good dish, a fine painting, a beautiful woman, a pretty house. I have given them

> a taste for beauty. That was the best thing I had to pass on to them. Apart from that…
>
> Chairman of departmental Chamber of Notaries, western France, 2003

> The majority of children aged between three and 12, especially in the US but these days in France and Europe, spend more time in front of screens—TV, computer, video games, mobile phone—than with their parents, teachers or friends: more than five hours a day on average, against less than four with their teachers, less than three with friends … and barely over an hour with their parents. Interactivity has changed the relation with digital images, making it the closest and most intimate relationship most children have, as well as the most comfortable, since it dispenses with direct human relations. The parade of feelings, emotions, adventures that can be summoned to the screen on demand is experienced more often and more intensely, with greater satisfaction, than anything off-screen. Reality is under new management; relation itself needs support from the digital, the all-purpose medium, so aptly symbolized by the silent couples one sees in trains and aircraft, linked only by their earphones plugged into the same CD or DVD player, communing through the same device with the generalized absence.

Bankers, insurers, asset managers were the first to benefit from the wealth of senior citizens and their growing (and justified) tendency to pass on their property, or at least supervise its transmission, under the best conditions, even when necessary by leapfrogging their children's generation to the advantage of their grandchildren. Gifts of shares, gifts of reversionary ownership, breaking up estates, out in the open, life insurance contracts in euros, discreetly invisible, or in units of account, highly visible… A whole specialized engineering—fiscal, social, family, patrimonial—has been set up in this area; it is even establishing the conditions for recognition of a new profession in the French financial galaxy: adviser in inheritance management, duly sanctioned by a diploma (CGPS). Life insurance organizes the patrimonial inclusion of bonds unknown to Napoleonic family law. Gifts of shares in property with reversionary ownership and retained usufruct favour transmission without transfer, but with a tax saving. Gifts by parents to children and grandparents to grandchildren accumulate to reduce the impact of wealth or inheritance taxes and speed up the movement of capital, avoiding transmission from elderly retired people to younger retired people (in France, a child still having both parents and all four grandparents can receive up to 360,000 euros completely free of inheritance tax, and up to 500,000 euros if his great-grandparents are still alive!). Transmission is becoming a voluntary act, a commonplace piece of management, an act of fiscal, social and family optimization. Professions are being formed to look after it. Because the growth of the sums to be transmitted is permanent, like that of the resulting commissions. The fact is that the circulation of inheritances is becoming a national cause … a cause of growth. Fear of the future continues to inhabit the elderly and the very old for whom saving money means saving themselves, retaining power over things and over people.

The transmission industry is going well. That means that transmission itself is going badly being thus concentrated on inessentials, and having abandoned to the market what used to be a matter of faith, blood and ties. That means that transmitting is all over, as the family, school, army, church or party used to do it. Money alone circulates between the generations. It alone is invested with that duty of transmission that otherwise would not or could not be done for lack of institutions, for lack of plans, for lack of legitimate authority. A great deal of money is transmitted only because nothing else is transmitted any more, and the money is a poor substitute. The advent of the body as unique asset, as sole patrimony, calls into question the need to learn and the capacity to teach, at the same time ruining the institutions of transmission and their perilous duty of linking generation with generation over time, which asks only to be undone, lost, forgotten. For the legitimacy of teaching, and of transmitting, is fading away now that the usefulness of knowledge, belief in progress and the value of distinctness are no longer there. It means too that family ties have gone elsewhere, the same elsewhere as the gods, the father and the master.

The pursuit of liquidity, everywhere and in everything, is destructive of transmission, hostile to the delays, the permanence, the security that it requires. And the spectacular growth in the average size of estates, in France and throughout Europe, needs to be taken into account, along with its counterpart, an accelerated liquidation of the codes, values and rules that used to make society. This financial enrichment should be understood as the counterpart of a liquidation of the family that has made a majority of French children born in the 1980s and 1990s rich and isolated children, and no one's children.

There are few examples suggesting the contrary. Outside its commonplace form, reduced to monetary and financial terms, it is becoming increasingly difficult to organize any sort of transmission. Between the generations, time seems to have frozen. The more money is passed on, the more the transmission process seizes up. There is more money being passed on, because nothing else is being passed on any longer ... or rather, the increase in the transmission of money corresponds to an exceptional phase of liquidation of non-monetizable structural assets. Just as the recent phenomenon of tyrannical children—who, as worthy objects of desire (you wanted to have me, so do your duty...), demand everything, right now, from their submissive parents—results from the wish of parents to seduce instead of command, from the mother's choice to please and caress rather than teach, the father's to retreat or indulge instead of discipline, so the inflation of the sums of money inherited with the parents' blessing should be understood as reparation and as a substitute for the transmission that has not been and will not be made ... value is transmitted because values have not been. School, family, army, church, nation ... the institutions that used to frame that transmission, giving the ties between different selves the depth of history, have withdrawn, are holding back, or find themselves baffled by a task whose very conditions have deteriorated. The new element is that the difficulty of relating, the erasure of the father, the scrambling of parental roles behind the compulsory satisfaction of the children, are depriving a growing number of children of what enables them to grow and mature: lack and rules. In France there are 600,000 adolescents whose lives have gone off the rails through early obesity, drink or drugs, suicidal impulses and seriously asocial behaviour, casualties of the breakdown in transmission afflicting the West for the last 30 years.

The money is not there for ornament. On the contrary, the child is the object of continuously rising expenditure. What is true of parents' spending on their children, which emerges from a steadily improving standard of living—how many children's schooldays are passed in the freezing classrooms and dormitories of yesteryear, how many sleep three to a room at home, now that a room for every child, equipped with a TV or computer screen, passes for the norm?—is equally true of collective spending, so-called 'national' education and culture being openly prioritized despite an admitted absence of convincing results. The purchase of toys, presents, interfaces is intended to provide children with the instruments of the repertoire they will have to perform, by buying what is not transmitted; in a way that is astonishingly differentiated between boys and girls, and astonishingly adult too, as if the first effect of the cult of childhood were an interdiction on being a child. But all that is being spent in this process is money; parents and children have been spending less and less time together over the last 50 years. After the development of childhood schooling, now compulsory, transmission has been shared—not without rivalry and argument—between the parents, at home, and outside teachers, representatives of the state or the church rather than of learning. This sharing arrangement was upset when the screen stopped being the mediator of reality and became reality itself. And it is upset at the very time that what is transmitted from generation to generation is being reduced to money, since nothing else (for lack of time, lack of confidence, lack of pride) can be transmitted. While the average size of inherited estates is still increasing (in France, it exceeded 100,000 euros in 2004, while the average size of all estates was below 60,000 euros), social, structural capital is not transmitted, or only in part, and is not inherited. Because although people want to transmit only that in which they can take legitimate pride, and that is recognized by society, the breakdown in transmission is foreseeable, indeed already manifest in public expressions of shame and embarrassment with the self, and only its consequences remain to be established.

You have to belong to be defined; to have been constrained to feel your freedom; to have felt want to live out your desires. You have to be sure of what you have, proud of what you have and strong in what you are to transmit it. And you have to accept what you are, your provenance and lineage, really to inherit; for every inheritance is a debt that its beneficiaries should honour. For many centuries the whole field of transmission was occupied by the dialogue between land and death, with its succession of new beginnings, its anecdotes and dramas ... but very few surprises. For centuries, the roles of the mother and father, of the established order, of frustration, of difference, drove children out of the household and enabled them to choose their own similar path. The ancestors were heroes, the parents their witnesses. Not entirely true perhaps, but a good story well worth believing. We do not have that helpful advantage. The culture of guilt, of being ashamed, has jammed the machine for turning out models that was also an integrating and transmitting machine, sheltered from an unhesitatingly assertive authority. How can parents to whom so much has been said about the mediocrity of their lives, their choices, their votes and history, continue to feel the pride essential for the transmission of what they have and the reproduction of what they used to be? How can parents so thoroughly trained in being ashamed of themselves by the reconstruction of the 1950s, by decolonization and the financial revolution of the 1970s, manage to pass on what made them who they are? The wasting away of structural capital in Europe, in the West, plays an underlying role behind the wreckage of adolescence, the difficulty of childhood, that now call in question the consequences of the family models and parental roles invented by the moral generation, its invocation of so many virtues to produce so much unnoticed misery.

That loss of the self is not without financial effects. The French used to pass on everything they could and consume as little as possible. Even today their level of saving, exceptionally high in Europe and the wider world at around 15 per cent of disposable income (rising to 18 per cent at the end of 2003!), shows the gap that separates the French from the consumer society. Horror of the speculator husband, the gambling addict husband, the ruined wastrel, has long haunted the imagination of bourgeois families.

This stereotype has now disappeared from the family unconscious. A first revolution occurred around 20 years ago, when death stopped being the precipitating event for the transmission of patrimony, now to be managed in anticipatory fashion by donation, by manual gift, by jumping a generation. The fiscal concessions recently granted to parent–child or grandparent–grandchild donations are merely the most recent episodes in a quest for economic efficiency, legitimate in itself, but dismissive of the situations of debt that arise within families and the dependences, the interests, the haggling—and also the conflicts—that can result from them. We need to be ready for a second revolution in succession and transmission: the French are going to pass on what they choose to pass on, and they are going to consume what they can, all that they can, all that is left once the management of their bequests has been completed, increasingly early, in increasingly optimized form, and with increasing restraint and precision. The transmission of money and property is changing as violently as that of knowledge and social practices; the arrival at retirement age of the children of the baby boom, now in their fifties, will witness a break in the order and nature of transmission, and also in the amounts involved. This transformation is driven less by an egotistical turning in on the self than by a sort of vertigo: what is transmission for? Or even: is there any point in leaving anything?

A first stage is being crossed by those young retired people who think in terms of passing on only what they have been left by their parents, just that and no more; considering the rest, the fruit of their own work, deals and risk-taking, to be their own property, underpinning the quality of their lives. This tendency affects the size of the estates being passed on and alters relations between the generations. But it does not end the chain of transmission that unites them.

A second stage is being started by those who feel themselves freed of all responsibility for the rising generations once they have provided their own children with a complete education, a professional training of high standard; once they have passed on that social capital that, in market-based societies, constitutes a fortune in itself, or the promise of fortune at least. Choosing and paying for a private school, financing further education, with courses abroad or a US master's degree, a leg-up in the early stages, the first job; tutoring in self-presentation, how and when to say their piece, teaching that code of courtesy that is also reserve, a weapon and a shield ... knowing how to appreciate a wine or a dish, to negotiate an encounter, judge a show, enjoy a place visited, is an asset beyond price, that might be called distinction, whose transmission may be more determining in the course of a life than that of more tangible assets. There is no doubting the material reality of the investment: to pay someone's way through a leading business school, a good engineering school or a prestigious MA or MSc costs tens of thousands of euros a year. But the labour market can repay the investment in salary over the first five years of employment, even show a gain. Nor is there any doubting the investment of time, attention and energy needed to inculcate codes, rituals, modes of address and discourse and the self-confidence given by education. Quite the opposite of the forced socialization of crèche and nursery school, training in distinction often mobilizes the mother, or the father, at home, demands individual attention and personal motivation; but this transmission pays too, by implanting some of those social markers that can have decisive, even overwhelming importance, in the absence of competition in learning, through objective and anonymous validation of knowledge and skills. This family transmission has become central to the lives of children or grandchildren; it might even seem that such immaterial transmission is coming to play the role that transmission of the house, land or deposit account played until recently, but now only plays in a marginal or indirect way.

And should we be expecting, even in France, a third stage, in which liberalization of spending on the body and living persuades people to pay a great deal, to pay everything—to the point of ruining estates, liquidating property and subjecting the whole economy to an explosion of spending on long life and favouring the body—merely to prolong life, or make it more bearable, for another year, another month, even another week? It is not yet a matter of free individual choice, not so much for lack of interest as for lack of opportunity, limited by the supervisory presence of the institutions, the mediation of doctor, hospital or medical expenses claim form. But the irresistible rise of social debt (in France, under CADES[7]) does suggest that the tendency is a lasting one. In the near future, on an open health and well-being market, a bid market, there will be nothing to prevent individuals from behaving like the authorities and piling up social debt year after year, the better to serve the present.

Without being aware of it, without meaning to, that last generation is fabricating a first generation—the first generation without parents, without friends, without ties—and leaving it with an unnoticed debt, that of producing and buying in the form of commercially supplied services what the family, parenthood, neighbourliness, proximity and tradition used to dispense free of charge. It is establishing an inequality between the generations that demography has never allowed in the past. And it is organizing misfortune for the growing numbers of old people, whose only positive representation of themselves is the inaccessible ideal of youth, as well as for the young, held increasingly remote from money, power and reality itself, dispossessed of their future and even their dreams.

From self-hatred to self-loss

From all of that too, family, institutions, neighbourliness, tradition, we have been liberated. By paying. Reducing the definition of all assets to their financial value trivializes them and absolves us of any obligation to them. The general growth of prosperity marginalizes concern with passing on the estate in comparison with other factors, when indeed it does not free elders from any obligation to their descendants: everyone has to make his own way in life. And anyway, these days, 'it's only money'. Through long resignation to being merely what they have, and also because they have been filled with guilt, misled into feeling ashamed of themselves,

7. Translator's note: CADES is the Caisse d'Amortissement de la Dette Sociale, a Social Security Debt Repayment fund that finances the debt accumulated by the French national security scheme from 1994 to 2006.

despising their way of life, their memories and regrets—and what anti-French campaigns have come from *Amélie* (dir. Jean-Pierre Jeunet, 2001) or *Les Choristes* (dir. Christophe Barratier, 2004)!—Europeans have let their inability to transmit show in their denial of history, and in their devaluation of the structural capital they are forgetting to feel proud of, because they have forgotten that it is what makes them rich.

The result is a strange situation in which the generations cohabit increasingly, and the forms of relation between them are becoming disorganized to allow everything while structuring nothing; and in which, most importantly, ever more watertight cultural frontiers are determined by generational limits. Family rituals used to organize communication and maintain relations in a way now neglected, what with the recomposition of partnerships, dissociation from descent and lineage and the decline of communal living. A sporting grandfather and his grandson are physically more comparable, and at the same time more distinct in their musical, sexual, sartorial and social references, than they have ever been in the past. What might be called a generational partitioning is appearing, as inside each generation a whole universe of sound, atmosphere, ritual, colour, body language and so on is assembled, shared, coherent and totally opaque to other generations. Same films, same pin-ups, same music, same favourite dishes, same sartorial flourishes, same range of self-images, same professional role models, a large majority of adolescents and young adults have far more in common with each other than with anything they may share with their parents and elders. And they resemble one another more and more closely, from Paris to Hong Kong, San Francisco to Delhi or Kuala Lumpur no doubt, anyway from Naples to Berlin and Paris to Lisbon, certainly more closely than they resemble their parents. Same night-time haunts, same drinks and products, same rhythms, same sounds and same states of awareness at raves or parties, same cult of well-being and self-image… The role of planetary brands and of the media, of information technology and the internet, appears to be determining in a development establishing planetary referents at the very beginning of the twenty-first century, breaking the solidarity between generations based on common territory, kinship and culture to recreate a worldwide appetite for inter-generational fusion, in a joyous and consequence-free cross-breeding and a reflex, unconscious submission to the market.

A variety of reasons, not all obvious, explain this phenomenon, characteristic of the rise of a global society, coinciding with the dream of a democratic planet. The most determining element undoubtedly resides in the changed status of the child, which upsets in its turn that of property and its transmission. The fact that parenthood emerges from sexuality, and therefore from the couple, underlies a transformation which is just beginning. Sexual desire no longer has anything to do with procreation; desire for a child no longer has any connection with sexual desire. A child is no longer the fruit of its parents' desire for each other, it is the fruit of their desire for a child, when it is not the mere exercise of a right, as for example in countries that permit child adoption by homosexual couples. On this point too the break with the physical bodies of the man and woman, to the advantage of an indeterminate juridical, political and contractual body, is decisive. The expression 'natural child' used to designate children resulting from an illicit sexual liaison outside the bonds of marriage, threatening to disturb the transmission of property by giving rise to moral rights not covered by family law, and feared for that reason by orderly lineages: it threatened the order of inheritance. The term is disappearing from our vocabulary not because of a resurgence in the sanctity of marriage, but because no child will be born in future following an accidental encounter, through passion or by accident; every child will be born out of the desire for a child of its parents … or parent. There will be no more natural children, because nature will have nothing to do with the conception of a child. It could be that the partitioning of generations is intended primarily to protect the child against excessive desire, too burdensome or stifling, since it knows that it fulfils a desire; and transmission is certainly upset as a result. The wish for a child, the decision to have one, then the costs and responsibilities of education and preparation for life, drain the will to transmit … and anyway, what more can they decide to leave, who have already decided to bestow life? It is as if the arrival of procreation in the field of will, of choice, of the administration of a life-plan, made it unnecessary to give more. In these conditions, a technical change—assisted, then industrial procreation—would create an explosive political situation, and a historic breakdown of transmission in Europe.

Substitution of ties

The steady increase in pension levels, the even more spectacular growth of returns on financial investments, three quarters of which are held by people over 60 in Europe, justify the substitution of commercial services for things done free of charge by the family. For wealth separates people, enrichment isolates; it is up to each generation to get ready to look after itself. It is time to have done with a liturgy of inter-generational solidarity that works, in reality, in the opposite way to the one it claims: the most protected get increased protection from it, while those suffering the rigours of competition, the market and the environment suffer them even more. And it would be useful to clarify the mechanism that results in pensioners acquiring political and financial muscle from high dividends levied on companies in the competitive sector, and therefore on the labour of their children and grandchildren, sometimes demanding enough to deprive them of the peace of mind, energy, spare time and money they would need to look after their parents or elders. The effects of a financial interdependence in which 60 per cent of the dividends earned by big French companies serve as pension payments, via the pension funds, while 10 per cent of their turnover, before tax, serves to cover dividend distribution, are the opposite of living solidarity. Their by-products are isolation and the substitution of the market for the institution, with contracts replacing bonds and prices instead of relations.

What the family, village or educational establishment offered free of charge but in an individually restricting way, is offered by our market companies in a way that is individually chosen but financially profitable. For the bond established by provision of gratuitous services has been broken, along with those of descent and origin. The tripling in the number of single mothers in France over three decades (650,000 in 1968, 1,900,000 in 2004) says as much as the number of divorced or separated adults, seven or eight million today, who are raising three million children and supply around half of schoolchildren needing special academic help (three to four times the proportion coming from stable two-parent families). And the deepening confusion between family law intended, essentially through marriage, to organize descent, in other words civil status, and a law of the individual expected to guarantee everyone the freedom not only to get what they can out of life but to use others, including children, to that end, undermines the conditions for transmission: acceptance of the order of time, life and death.

A French teacher and his whole class of pupils, in the 1950s, would have been able to discuss Racine or Corneille with Alain's class from the 1920s,[8]

8. Translator's note: Alain, born as Émile-Auguste Chartier (1868–1951), French philosopher.

or Jules Lemaître's around 1860,[9] or lycée pupils in the Empire's schools from 1810; probably they would not have been all that put out by the philosophers of the Enlightenment and the Encyclopaedia. Rome and Athens were theirs; their grandfathers, their masters, were as close to them as anyone. Now we have done away with Latin and Greek, along with masters of all sorts. After all, what more do they have to tell us than a rapper from LA, a Kabyle singer or a Jamaican reggae survivor? The dissolution of forms, the suppression of the aesthetic aspects of human relations, the setting at arm's length of individual passions, is laying the groundwork for incomprehension of what made great Western art: religious figures, dramas of passion, the exclusivity of human love relations, adventures of the individual facing destiny, duty, loyalty, attachment. Even the most secular of 1950s arts teachers would not have doubted it; any of his French pupils would have recognized a station of the Cross, a Resurrection of bodies or a naked Venus. From Giotto to Racine, Shakespeare to Delacroix, very soon there will be no more meaning to be drawn from a history that is no longer ours and feelings that are no longer ours, to which the keys have been lost.[10] In the religious domain, the same break is occurring in a much more violent way: between what France was in the 1960s and what Europe is in 2010, between France in 2005 and what the US is threatening to become.[11] Even children at private Catholic schools, even the offspring of the most traditionalist families in Versailles or Quimper, will react with blind incomprehension to any representation, the word of any parent or grandparent, trying to convey what religious festivals used to be like in a Norman or Breton village, what a wayside altar signified during the big parades in May, or the feast of Corpus Christi, when the local authorities, from the prefect to the head of the Gendarmerie or local army general walked in procession behind the cathedral banners, singing 'Catholiques et français toujours'. That world of certainty, faith and self-assurance, that carried a mediaeval City of God all the way through to the second half of the twentieth century, in which God was the be-all and end-all of existence, is no more and will never be seen again in that form; is no more except in what is known as Muslim fundamentalism, which is simply what a religion is when it remains all that a religion is; something you can kill for, something you can die for.

9. Translator's note: François Élie Jules Lemaître (1853–1914), French writer and drama critic.

A return to pride in what we are and an ambition to mature is the precondition for a new accumulation of structural capital. We have all the necessary means, more the means perhaps than a clear idea of what to do with them. It would be a pity though if the generation associated with the end of history, that invented the woman, that also invented the environment and the quality of life, should pass on without leaving any of its discoveries behind. The failure of that transmission would be equivalent to a liquidation, an unprecedented individual and collective loss that only a generation living as if it were the last, detached from all future generations and any idea of collective duty, could contemplate without flinching. For the Word and the self are transmitted through the rule and death. You have to know how to obey to be able to die. But the children consumed by their parents' desire for a child, the children produced by the body market now extending its empire and becoming universal, escape the dominion of the rule and death by entering the world of consumption, production and the market. And how could Europe think of carrying on, if European society dispensed with the rule and refused death? The last generation with its society wants to get out of passing on the rule and talking about death; it wants to prevent its children from becoming themselves, to stop them from growing up. The breakdown of death that is now ageing Europe is stopping its children from building, from taking their place in the chain of generations, giving and receiving, as their due and not by legal right, in belonging and in freedom. And the extraordinary abeyance in which Europe finds itself is congealing in a hope that it might never end, that it will never have to transmit, never have to acknowledge the father, the other, the rule, error and death.

Towards the dominion of sterile life?

The main achievement of Western civilization at the end of the last century is sterility. It presides over the break in transmission as a buried dream, as economics in action and as shameful satisfaction.

The revolution launched by the contraceptive pill during the 1960s, by way of the desired, proclaimed, ideological dissociation between sex and conception, extended its effects all over the planet. It is putting an end to the exuberant prodigality of human life. Children used to be synonymous with wealth to come, seen as a blessing and an advance. But despite the reassuring nature of advertising discourse, they came to be seen as what makes you old before your time, burdensome, costly, to be avoided. The demographic transition in the developed countries between one generation and the next, where a chosen, lower birth rate already insufficient to ensure renewal of the generations has succeeded an explosive birth rate leading to many generations of massive population growth, is reaching all parts of the world. China has already embarked on a demographic regression that India, Malaysia and the Maghreb should enter in less than a generation. The astonishing thing is not that, for the first time in history outside periods of war, rich countries wallowing in all that progress can offer are in demographic decline; what is astonishing is that countries that have something to gain, that need to progress and develop, are galloping even faster down the same path. Sterility has become a sign of development, a token of higher consumption levels.

So that the brutal question of the exhaustion of essential resources is being replaced by the more subtle one of the sort of societies people will inhabit in 30, 40 or 100 years' time. And so that the economics of scarcity, the politics of resources, are being quietly replaced by an economics of desire and a politics of the body, clothed in terms like 'well-being' and 'quality of life', but also a morality governing the relation with the self and the relation with nature. And lastly, so that demography is and will become increasingly the science that illuminates all the others, and that contains them … or contains us. Demography is unloved among the human sciences. No doubt because it is protestant by birth. Because it speaks of all that remains to us of nature, which still determines us and will continue doing so for the foreseeable future, to wherever imagination can lead us; it is the science of bodies that are born and that are going to die. And if death is all that still lives in nature, if exorcizing nature is a convulsive effort to delay, deny or forget death, then demography too is something that has to be denied, hidden and forgotten.

For the human species is mortal like all the others, and will remain so. And the European species, which made this world what it is, will have vanished from it by the end of this century. Just as that great creature the blue whale, despite conservation measures effectively banning its capture for several decades past, still wanders the southern oceans but no longer reproduces, just as those Leviathans, which haunted the imagination of seagoing peoples since prehistory, have chosen to let themselves die, to leave a world that no longer has a place for them in its dreams and myths, so we may imagine Europeans in their unconscious wisdom choosing to resign from a world that has escaped them. Perhaps behind the syndrome of the last generation there lies a very strong feeling of the end of something that used to be called man, that was from this land, this Europe, this Atlantic promontory, and that the end of nature, the advent of the body and the dominion of sterile life have made that man permanently redundant, but for what?

4. The Body's Politics

The body has taken power. Behind the changes stirring European and American societies, and now Asian ones too, the advent of the body is at work, pressing its advantages, its progress made all the more irresistible by the adoption of a variety of masks: human rights, openness, development... However, in the world concert that is one of the visible faces of what we call globalization, Europe is distinct. In its chosen interpretation, Europe has embarked on a singular adventure that is distancing it from its allies and perhaps from itself: asserting the freedom of the individual in relation to everything—religion, family, tribe, nation, origin—that determines him. To that end it has had to repress or destroy those intermediary bodies, the structures that subjected the individual to the collective by threatening his survival, and the more determining forms that gave him an identity, distinguished his immediate circle from others, the near from the distant, and thus protected him from isolation, or from himself. And also to valorize the shift, ensure the reversibility of all undertakings, keep the network fluid, by destroying institutions and renouncing all connections. So that what used to be ours, by way of forms and rules, is now extended to the rest of the world, without distance or difference excluding anyone... Killing geography with the market, the law and rules.

The disappearance of the sacred, along with the religion that used to administer it, is not unconnected with the advent of the body. All of that is already over and done with. What is still going on is the disappearance of history, along with the politics that was supposed to bring about the advent of history in society. The advent of the body inverts the time-honoured order of priorities that dedicated the body of every man and woman firstly to the perpetuation of the species, secondly to the defence, and if possible the progress, of their community. The tempos of the body marked the responses to that vocation; having children and perpetuating the lineage, taking up arms to defend frontiers, passing on rituals, codes of recognition, memory and tradition to the young, all placed the body in the service of the group. For the first time in the existence of homo sapiens, a majority of adults in the West are either too old to reproduce, or no longer want to. And for the first time in the history of a world that is what Europe has made it, most Europeans doubt the reality of progress, want no singing tomorrows and are not prepared to fight to increase their power. The politics arising from this anthropological transformation is working an almost complete, albeit paradoxical, inversion: inversion of private and public, inversion of the dominion of the rule and that of the bond, above all inversion of a relation that now subordinates the collective to the body, to the individual, to everyone. The only meaning the group, the social, the law still possess is their meaning to my body, its satisfaction, its youth, its long life. Almost a complete inversion, but paradoxical, in so far as it leaves the question of means without an answer, while suggesting that by developing these demands it is courting ruin.

This European take on the advent of the body is much conditioned by the lessons of the long and arduous twentieth century. We have learned to distrust leaders, opinion-formers and rabble-rousers. We are experienced in the suspicion that should greet every grand plan, every shining vision. Most probably we should not stop at abandoning singing tomorrows, but should give up meaning altogether … how scandalous it seemed on this side of the Atlantic, George W. Bush apparently believing in evil and lining America up with good! Those who claim that the words 'progress', 'future', or 'growth' have meaning and give direction are inaudible to deafened Europeans; for their most ambitious enterprises caused such ruin and suffering in the last century! Hence, the passion to disconnect the individual from the collective; hence also the worsening European blindness to the conditions that would allow the history of national self-determination among the nations comprising the Union to continue, starting with the military preconditions for power and freedom.

Politics used to subject bodies and lives to a common destiny or ideal; politics now must submit to the varied, fleeting and capricious destinies we give to our own lives. The act is sufficient in itself, for those who perform it, if it satisfies them, if it augments their self-awareness, broadens their experience and sharpens their perception. Doubtless the advent of the body also marks another, deeper break, a break between the act and its meaning, between hope and progress, between the local and the global, a break that enjoins politics to rid itself of any aspiration to meaning or destiny.

Liberate everyone from fear, need, danger; free everyone from the family, the community, from all that binds, retains, weighs down, holds back; the advent of the body legitimizes politics in the body's service, places its satisfaction, its activity, its enjoyment over all that might only be means to those ends: law, rules, society, kinship. So that while there has indeed been a revolution, it was not the one predicted, not the one that continues to be cited like a password, the reality revolution. The body used to be the instrument of God, master, lord or emperor, its destiny to be battered in war or bent to the machine or the plough; the body used to be a tool that reason applied in the quest for progress and the construction of a better world. Now it is the master and judge of its own satisfaction, its enjoyment, and convenes the world with its learning and laws to further those ends. In the process, and as if through carelessness, in Europe at least, it is casually overturning the old categories of public and private, blurring the outlines of the self and the other, and trying to deny that the near and the distant still have meanings.

This tendency remained more or less hidden from those looking in the places where history used to be made: assemblies, policy programmes, major national debates, ideologies… Sounds, rhythms and vibrations say a lot more about it than politicians' speeches; the Rolling Stones, Jimi Hendrix and the Doors were more political than Richard Nixon, Georges Pompidou and Edward Heath. Screens, digital technologies, mobile phones have changed life more than any politician could. For technology has made revolution in bodies, not in assemblies. The separation between the emotional and the rational, between the imagination of the West and its political truth, have counted for more than laws, organizations and institutions. But it is not surprising that the development that transformed reality should have stayed hidden. For it imposed itself from below, in societies that had become porous, and that had undertaken to ignore their frontiers and sacralize individual life. It was brought about by tools and processes, without ever being stated or published. The advent of the body is carried by the techniques that place the world at the body's disposal. In the process, these techniques dispense with any obligation to belong, to be represented, to debate and vote. The institutions, along with tradition, transmission, the senses themselves, are turned upside down; and not just turned upside down, but (some of them at least) sidelined altogether. Instructions for use make democratic debate redundant; the market supplants parliament, price determines the law, management of identities replaces frontiers, individual coding dispenses with belonging and nationality. So that the foundations of democracy as we continue to articulate and operate it are disappearing without work on the structures and forms that will replace them even being started, let alone completed. The democratic planet is without discourse.

Its traces must be sought to provide a narrative, a history and place of remembrance, for a development that became more necessary the longer the evidence for it was hidden, and its effects continued to animate us. Just as much as private prosperity and withdrawal from nature and labour, turning our backs on war, the nation, the order of the self and the bond, changes bodies and questions what society is made of. We believe we have seen the last of war, the foreigner, the enemy. But it is society which is vanishing, society which used to assign everyone to a place, fix destinies and guide lives. And along with frontiers, separate currencies, origins, it is our certainties that are being erased, what we have in common that is receding, leaving everyone with their own body as ultimate frontier and last society. For what with the exhaustion of group narratives, the great fatigue that descends on the mind at the thought of seeking historical truth, or the truth of nature or matter, only the narrative of the body, its satisfaction, its pleasure, and the quest for new registers of sensibility, experience and emotion, still retain our attention. Our system of truth, which is that of the market, enjoins us to believe that everything can always be negotiated, that all we need to do is pay for everything, even for peace, and even for good.

In many ways, this condition could be considered a simple extension of the intellectual, moral and political revolution driven by technology that, in the seventeenth century, brought about an 'anthropological revolution'[1] launching the transformation, domestication and then subjection of nature by man, and putting labour and usefulness in the place where God, the king or fate had assigned an immobile and comforting place to every individual. What that would mean in short would be following the same path into another domain and intensifying it through new means. But this is not so. It is no longer a matter of applying the resources of mind, the economy and method to the outside, to the look; it is about producing humans. Not about making God, nature, tradition and the ancients redundant, as the moderns dreamed of doing, and as the French Revolution lied by not doing; just as much about not embracing or renouncing any aspect of the future, but freezing an immobile present. No longer a matter of merely organizing productive activities in a profitable manner,

1. See Jean Rohou, *Le Débat*, 130, May 2004.

but mobilizing all available means, even into the future, in the service of satisfaction and well-being. No more constructing, building, founding; just rhythm, speed and movement. On the spot. In a residence in place, provided by the hidden capital we have accumulated without knowing it, that we are consuming without counting the cost, and that will run out ... what once made society between the peoples of the West, and is now receding. In this transformation, which is bringing sex into the law, which is inventing a new moralism, which is handing the body over to politics, what used to be called freedom, democracy, the state, are at risk.

After indeterminate man—the man without qualities—comes man without society.

The Republic's sex

In the history of the body in politics, of bodies in society, the astonishing thing is not the change that inverts the relation between emotion and reason, image and discourse, and gives birth to the economics of sensation, biological intelligence and the politics of emotion. What is astonishing is that this historic seizure of power from the public by the private should have occurred in France, and in an unexpected area: that it should have emerged from the most private domain possible, the bedroom, in a country where, for the 300 years since the Treaty of Westphalia, everything that counted had happened on the main stage of government, of power and nations, and for the two centuries since the Industrial Revolution, everything that counted came from the economy.

The May 1968 crisis, which was to end the historic compromise between Communism and Gaullism in France and force the US to seek an urgent exit from Vietnam, began with the demand for free access by students of both sexes to the sleeping quarters of their segregated halls of residence. The demand led to vigorous student heckling of the French education minister, François Misoffe, during a visit to Nanterre. His suggestion that a nice cold bath would calm people down was not just stupid, but revealed a surprising ignorance of history as it was then being made on campus, in cinemas and in bedrooms. Not for moralistic reasons—at other times, General de Gaulle had shown a lordly indifference to the sexual preferences of his associates, provided he knew nothing about them—more through blindness to the sudden intrusion of sex into the field of law, the public stage and power. And through a deluded view of the territory of politics, already being invaded by unknown groups of ministers with names like the Beatles and the Rolling Stones, some of whom would soon be thought more famous than Jesus. Soon after that, the musical *Hair* would be the first to show performers naked on stage; in California, 'Flower Power' would breach the walls of American puritanism with its own historic assertion of public nudity, although with a very different destiny.

Thirty or 35 years on, the French minister's remark would be inconceivable. Because what used to stay in the bedroom is on posters, on walls and on TV. And because sexual relations, the modalities of desire and satisfaction—solitary, in couples, threesomes or more, heterosexual or homosexual—have surged hungrily into the world of law, of courts and verdicts, and are hammering at the door of electoral debate, edging towards inclusion in campaign posters and matrimonial law. In a spectacular somersault, what was originally presented as the absolute antidote to the family, marriage and bourgeois convention now aspires to nothing less than its own subjection to those same conventions and that same institutional—and fiscal—status. For the whole of the art of politics has become a matter of encouraging enjoyment—of food, sex, sport—or facilitating it, justifying it, confirming and validating it, just as the primary function of competing firms is to invent desire. The real meaning of the student revolt at Nanterre and the '22nd March movement' was nowhere near the barricades in the Latin Quarter; it was in the draft bill tabled by the courageous Lucien Neuwirth in 1967 leading—after what debates!—to a law legalizing the sale of the contraceptive pill, finally voted through in 1974 under the so-called 'Veil' law on voluntary termination, the right to abortion on demand.

At the end of these major developments in the laws of morality and the law on bodies, accompanied of course by steadily hardening attitudes to rape and child abuse and a strengthening of child protection laws, the law left the domain of politics and the collective (favouring demographic growth) to enter that of personal lifestyle (guaranteeing freedom of sexual relations, giving free expression to sexual minorities). Since then, from Paris-plage to the Berlin Technoparade, in the multiplying gay pride demos and love parades in all the European capitals, the spectacle of enjoyment is everywhere, and even more the demand for it relayed, amplified and organized by a body politic whose sole horizon seems to be its own dissolution in the physical ecstasy of its participants.

The body, morality and death

In a perfect echo of May 1968 and free access by girls to boys' dorms, the hysteria that seized Western countries over the spread of Acquired Immune Deficiency Syndrome (AIDS) confirmed the position of sex at the centre of public life, along with the freedom to have sex with partners of one's choice, in conditions and employing the practices of one's choice, from the position of a social imperative absolute and coercive for all parties: taxpayer, insured, borrower, all being required to pay without saying a word for the consequences of sexual behaviour known to be 'risky', even and above all when it is alleged by some to be 'responsible'. The illness is not without equivalents, either in the number of cases (malaria kills more patients each year), or the difficulty of its diagnosis, or its fatal outcome; its wholly exceptional status originates primarily from the explosive marriage of blood, sperm and death, subsequently from the horrified reaction to the spectacle of death in the young and beautiful, desired and desirable, some socially visible—the dying Nureyev having himself carried backstage at the Opéra Garnier in Paris to be present at the performance of his last ballet!—and is finally the fruit of this inversion: everything private, everything secret about the body and its preferences, occupied the public arena for the first time, most especially in France where the contaminated blood scandal, beyond the public figures compromised by it, associated sex and death with power and money. AIDS and HIV have generated an audience for writers and broadcasters on sex, programme presenters and self-proclaimed experts; some of these, especially in radio (the Skyrock station) have been extraordinarily effective in attracting adolescents and young adults to fuel a permanent broadcast show featuring themselves, and reviving the ancient art of voyeurism with moral pretensions. Under extremely effective pressure from associations and organizations mobilized around this theme, a spectacular inversion has been worked, behind the embarrassed silence of a society trapped in its own compassionate discourse; what used to be done a lot more often and a lot better when no one talked about it has been written up, analyzed, evaluated, in order to be protected ... doubtless with all the more conviction since the desire fled from it. The clamorous demand for condom machines in secondary schools raised advertising of the relations between sex, death and the law to unprecedented levels. Not only in the public forum but in school playgrounds, in school textbooks, access to the body is through the genitals; for how many years will AIDS prevention classes remain the only teaching on preventive hygiene in French schools (still very backward in this area compared to other European countries, especially the Nordic ones)? The profusion of literature intended or professing to be sexological, dressed in all the panoply of analysis, pedagogy or prophylaxis, attests the strength of a shift that makes enjoyment a duty and its preconditions a right, and finds a sort of summit in the self-proclamation of Paris as the 'city of love'. What an age seems to have passed since the good doctor Zwang broke a taboo!

We have yet to measure some of the long-term effects of this shift. They include the ravaging force of a compulsory identification of sex with death (starting with secondary school courses on sexuality, which are essentially lessons in prophylaxis, based on the grim teaching that pleasure kills); the extraordinary power of the psychic images inspired by it; and the evident appearance of a new sexual puritanism in the images and words already being coined for the more recent figures of violent, absolute interdict, like paedophilia, sexual tourism or rape.

New epidemic, new governmental prosecutions, new setting for a daily act, private and sacred (because it too in its way produces life), and involving contact of the most intimate kind between the body and what is external to it: eating became a risk when the first cases of BSE (bovine spongiform encephalopathy) were diagnosed and its transmission to humans was confirmed by the first deaths. Like sexual relations, the relation to food could produce death as well as life; the very idea was appalling, the more so because science played a part, transforming living tissue by making ruminants devour fodder containing meat slurry; this has not finished haunting us. So yet another break is confirmed with the cremation of dozens, then hundreds, then thousands of sheep carcases, followed by huge numbers of cattle, not because the animals are infected but because the maintenance of meat export markets demands it. All the principles and all the attentions devoted to the human body are extended into the principles and attentions focused on the environment as representation, spectacle and sumptuous deployment of wilderness; nevertheless they manage to accommodate absolute indifference towards such instrumentalized forms of life as domestic pets, plants and farm animals raised for food. At a time when the ability to develop human bodies of instrumental status seems achieved or imminent, that is something worth remembering.

Annexation of the private

> According to Salman Rushdie, the most significant indicator of the level of civilization reached by a society may be free access to pornography. It is an idea worth discussing, especially given the number of hits on X-rated websites from countries like Pakistan. It is worth discussing, given the way sexual frustration has ploughed its furrows of war and fanaticism back and forth through history, up to and including today's fundamentalist strains of Islam. It is worth discussing, given Europe's vivid awareness that all the learning and sense of duty, the elevated moral qualities built by many generations through the centuries on frustration, repressed desires and forbidden satisfactions ended by producing horrors—from Auschwitz to the Great Proletarian Cultural Revolution—never even remotely equalled by the effects of any vice, cupidity, envy or lust ... a lesson America has yet to learn from us. It is worth discussing as a focus of hysteria still at work in our societies: hysteria over the sex trade in Asian or Latin American countries, like the sacrilegious status newly attributed to rape—in France, punished more harshly than murder—ample proof surely that in this area as in others, nothing is self-evident. We have not seen the last of good and evil. It is just that their masks have changed. And Salman Rushdie's assertion is worth discussing as the key to the coming politics, the politics of satisfaction which is annexing bed, pleasure and partying, the better to limit expenditure of power, money and force.

The confusion of public with private is the mark of dictatorships, and the establishment of the privately owned body, shielded from politics by habeas corpus, was a great English achievement at a time when the pillory, the lash, the gibbet and the treadmill still proclaimed in France the body's subjection to the public domain. The present growing confusion between the private and public domains rather suggests that we are moving away from politics as it has been defined since the agora and the forum: the business of the common good. Politics is becoming the art of serving particular interests, and in the first place ensuring the satisfaction of bodies. The privatization of politics is proceeding from that, with some unforeseen consequences: what meaning for example can the words 'equality', 'liberty', 'solidarity' still have in societies dedicated to the service of individual aspirations?

Those who consider that no civilization has tolerated women's sexual liberation for long, those who are observing with amused curiosity the emergence of a new moralism (the American students' associations whose members pledge chastity before marriage are one example), judge that we have gone well beyond merely noting the effect of AIDS on the generation whose adolescence came in the 1990s, for whom love was identified with sex, and sex with the condom: with suspicion of the other. The other means death; this is not a discourse that societies can promote with impunity.

Now that private sexual activity has become a public subject, now that scenes of sexual intercourse in cinema have become a commonplace—commonplace and public—representation of human relations, now that the demand of some homosexual couples to be married has publicized and even institutionalized the matter of sexual preferences, there is no longer any separation between the world of politics—public debate and decision, public laws and money—and the world of sexuality, enjoyment and the private. The first expression of this astonishing crossover has been the Republic's sex history, or how sex underlies some of the dominant developments in French democracy over the last 30 years. It is political at every stage, most notably in the growing gap being established between the US whose political assemblies, up to and including the White House, celebrate virginity in girls, marital fidelity and communal family prayers, and Europe, which is trying to forget the absurd indulgence with which it swallowed the teachings of bad masters presenting Mao's China, Stalin's USSR or Tito's Yugoslavia as desirable models for its own future, only to fly into a rage at the return of religion, history and direction in an ally it no longer understands. Enjoying one's own body until its dying day is becoming a theme of collective mobilization in Europe. The sexualization of society makes this demand irresistible and its public outcome inevitable; it will be the main vector for the transformation of hospices, residential homes and other retirement establishments. To gain acceptance, these antechambers to the grave are going to dress themselves up as short-time hostels; then society can applaud a conjuring trick that helps it to forget death.

The public discussion of the body's attitudes, positions and practices provides a foothold for the law, the rules, the standard and the contract: for convention. And it was through the liberation of morals that this shift began, that the body laid itself open: the liberation of morals made it extremely easy for the courts, the law and the authorities to enter a domain from which privacy and the institution of marriage formerly kept them at a distance. Forty years on, the effect, plainly, is that the private has become public. In support of pleasure, or to prevent it from disappearing, no amount of law, censorship or public money can be too much. Going to bed, eating, are objects of choice for government, for the law, and for image makers. The 'outing'—voluntary or forced—of homosexuals, required to admit what they were (and no longer what they did), officialized first the desire to 'confess', then the obligation. The campaign against risky driving behaviour, and the coming campaign against risky dietary practices, place the protection of the body, its well-being and its integrity, in the front rank of political priorities. So that the division between private and public, between personal choices and representations, has been replaced with exposure in the public forum and the inquisition preceding it; everyone is required to be what he or she does; and above all, everyone is required to bear a label. Behind the lesbian, gay and transsexual pride demonstrations, behind the celebration of the first homosexual marriages, behind the ideology of slimness, youth, toned muscle under the swimsuit, the frantic need for morality is obvious; it is not a matter of doing what one wants to do, but of saying so, of being recognized for that, even of being proud of it, of finding status in it. Never have sex and the identity card been so close together; nor, since the ancien régime (but using some of its means), has the socialization and judiciarization of bodies ever been as permanent, insistent and pervasive as it is now; indeed the invasion of the body by the law is becoming a formidable risk factor. For the law, with the body, has brought a market into existence, whose explosive growth is underlined among other things by the cost of insuring doctors against professional liability verdicts in the civil courts.

In the name of good

Nothing could be less anecdotal than this short history of bodies seized by the law, and politics seized by the body. Politicians used to live by healing the scars left by the last war while getting ready for the next one, always focused on the battlefield; in future they will have to keep an eye on the bed ... whether of confinement, hospital treatment or lovemaking. Another relation to the sacred, anyway an absolute, is taking shape here. The Catholic church in the US knows this better than most, having reached the brink of financial bankruptcy in 2004 through failure to understand that the sacralization of the body and genitals of the child could brook no weakness. The Archdiocese of Boston, which faces no fewer than 390 suits alleging paedophilia, is an example of the damage that will or may be suffered in the years to come by any institution or organization failing to anticipate the shift involving the takeover of sex by the law and the zooming in of public focus on the bed. Meanwhile the practice of whistle-blowing—public denunciation by privileged informants of reprehensible negligence in areas sensitive to public opinion—is becoming rapidly more popular, in private firms as well as public institutions.

Naturally, confession, judges and the law are no friends to desire. Naturally, as de Sade explained much earlier and better than the 'revolutionaries' of 1968, gratuitousness is the opposite of ecstasy. Naturally, in the back rooms of specialized establishments, you have to stake your life to come … protection, above all, means protection against desire. Naturally, behind the demand for sexual freedom there lay nothing, or very little; the only freedom lies in doing it, and collective political demonstration to that effect is lightweight stuff. And naturally, the opposite was advancing behind the slogans and banners: the opposite, meaning saturation, detachment, loss of interest brought about by the popularization of sex, by easy, gratuitous sex; the end of sex, finally, as an intoxication, as a red-hot iron, a goad. Loss of the ability to relate and reciprocally attract, the exhaustion of desire or, worse still, feeling ashamed of desire, ending in impotence and sterility, all proceed from the growing aggressiveness and omnipresence of the sexual discourse, and also in the end from its insignificance; for sexuality has become immaterial in the strict sense, unnecessary for the perpetuation of the human species. The time of the market has come, the time of the price, of the relation liquidated in the price; as a substitute, as a passage, as a disappointing dénouement to the great history of the sexes, desire and the law.

The politics of desire

> Give me desire,
> The desire to desire
> And reignite my life…
>
> Johnny Hallyday

Can excitement survive wealth? After the invention of the body and the assertion of its primacy, business and society are left with the primary function of the production of desire. Viagra symbolizes this pursuit of desire by the body, along with its essential rituals and self-interested servants. It used to be necessary to overcome the poverty of human products and means while overwhelmed by desire in a profuse world; what has to be overcome now is the disappearance of desire, its exhaustion in a world shrivelled by the excess of available means and techniques, the superabundance of products. It is not enough to note the technical possibility, tomorrow, very soon, of the production of life, production of the body; everything that resists the entry of that produced body to the market still has to be liquidated. It is not enough to dream of indeterminacy, to refuse transmission even subject to inventory, to cobble up identity and membership out of the junk-pile of cross-breeding; that body endowed with long life also has to be given the capacity to complete itself and eliminate all resistance to multiplying experiences. It is not enough to note, after organizing it, the disappearance of reality; a new world of rhythm, sensation, emotion, vibration, a world able to transport and enchant, will have to be recomposed. And, last but not least, it is not enough to recognize that abundance as a universal motivation and organizing principle can weaken the economy; circumstances have to be created to strengthen that motivation and that principle, and to reinstate them durably as representation and idea of the self; to recreate through desire the rarity that abundance threatens, the unsatisfied state that it satiates, and sell as a product what nature, society, institutions used to make available to all, or nearly all, outside the economy. For it is not enough to know that life is an asset; you still have to consume your life, to spend it ... or resign yourself to eternity as the richest stiff in the cemetery.

The desire system has no connection with the need system, either in psychology or in economics. On the contrary: the miracle of innovation is that, thanks to desire, it can set a high value—and thus a high price—on products or services that no one has ever needed, since they did not exist. The processes of innovation, of market creation, with which businesses foster their growth and feed their shareholders, remind us that both desire and frustration have to be invented to make people buy. The pressure of supply long since outweighed the logics of demand. So that inventing desire has become the main, obsessive, nagging work of business, the precondition for growth. Poverty and repression used to organize the economy of scarcity; now overabundance and enjoyment are going to organize the survival of the economy through sterility.

A political project involving an anthropological transformation is taking shape, as a means of pacification to surmount social tensions, a sublimation of the economy. The depiction of the body as an insatiable machine, a process and system, finds its finished expression in X-rated films and pornographic material, before moving on to video games—Sim City, Lara Croft, Grand Theft Auto—and their repertoire of forms and situations to swamp the imagination. With the opening in 1972 of *Deep Throat*—the first of George Damiano's pornographic films to get a commercial release—followed by the popular success of *Emmanuelle* (1974) and the aesthetically ambitious *Empire of the Senses* (1978), an industry was born (officially, in France, under the 1974 law on the release and exhibition of films under an X certificate). X-film imagery, increasingly commonplace in the mainstream, is not just a prosthesis to bridge the uncertainties of desire; it constructs a myth, replacing the real body—imperfect, satiated, tired—with the unsatisfied body of the market ... a new fairy story to dream away reality. Beyond the banal question of sexual excitation, which tends increasingly to supplant the difficult matter of relating by substituting an image of the body for the real body of another human, what is at work here is fascination with the idea of a body that is always ready for sex of every sort, in every possible position, with anyone, to arouse all desires and satisfy them without ever being satisfied itself. The X industry produces body in the abstract: sexless, odourless, untouchable, undifferentiated ... and without HIV or herpes; hence the magical, incantatory character of a growing, generalized consumption of the spectacle of the body fresh from its moult, something that long life, the production of life and the society of desire promise soon to make a reality. The obsessive repetitiveness of X imagery gives the most accurate picture of the self-programming body, both a terminal and a network, the body as a new figure for the infinite. Porn stars are the unconscious emblems of an economy whose chosen frontier is permanent non-satisfaction, whose engine is the body's unlimited disposition to desire; and of a politics that sees the release of all frustrations as an effective means of social pacification and a way to standardize behaviour; it is not surprising that the history of these specialized products, from furtive ghettos to the multinationals of digital internet sex (Vivendi International was the most powerful of these), is steadily taking its place as a history that counts, for it embraces a large part of the recent history of bodies, of models for the body and the way they are used. Nothing surprising either in the naïve heroicization of its actresses and actors—from Brigitte Lahaie to Ovidie—in their memoirs on the bookshop counter; they are the priests and priestesses of a cult, a cult of the body as non-satisfaction, as lack, as infinity. Nor is it astonishing that the development of the styles and content of specialized productions provides an invaluable lead for anyone wishing to cast light on the future of the society of bodies; invaluable, and sombre too.

The standardization of pleasure

> A text on sale for 2 euros in the stationery shelves of Monoprix stores in May 2005, entitled *More than Sex*, explained in the first few pages that a successful sexual relationship begins with individual masturbation by each partner in front of the other.

Popularized by the use in advertising of 'SM chic' and 'bobo[2] trash' images, embraced enthusiastically in 2002–3 by luxury brands like Gucci and Dior, the explosive alliance of sex and the market is characteristic of an economy desperate to produce desire, and that has to succeed in doing so if it is not to fall into static or negative growth. To that end, it has to fabricate a myth of the body, endow it with the dynamic of a model, and give moral primacy to its satisfaction. And it has to standardize pleasure. It used to be pleasant to have a good time; now it is virtuous. What the consumer society wants is not greater control over impulses but less, in particular less control over those impulses that increase and encourage desire. So that the language of subversion, of revolution, sung by the missionaries of rock and pop music, taken up by thinkers, filmmakers and artists and repeated in images and colours, should be read as a stream of effective sales pitches. So that those sexagenarian supergroups bashing away at their guitars for audiences of admen, consultants and bankers warming over the cold embers of their twenties, are guilty of no betrayal: they are just celebrating the satisfaction revolution they have achieved without knowing it. Their revolution may not be the one they expected, but what revolution ever is?

In an unusual inversion of public action, the structures that used to supervise, control and restrain the body, its excesses and risks, are becoming structures to incite, excite and provoke the body, its wishes and fulfilments. For nowhere in Europe is the question still one of investing, saving, showing restraint; the question posed by the behaviour of

2. Translator's note: bobo = 'bourgeois bohemian'.

Frenchmen and Europeans who are richer in property than desires, and in holdings than wishes, but who continue to save, is whether to permit spending, to unleash the wishes and desires that will generate fulfilment. Wishes, desires: the new economy is dedicated to giving them life. It propagates them, it upholds them as rules, against all the rules. It gives the name of liberation to what others would have called submission to desires, or to the injunction to have desires. It makes them into models for living. It is a mistake to think that in losing the old institutions, religion, frontiers, the family, we would be losing all structures; other structures, subtle enough to justify the expression 'invisible society', and perhaps for that reason more effectively meaningful, are there to provide guidance and direction, to accompany and orient the desires, wishes and tendencies of bodies. Where structures used to be seen as a hierarchy, supervised by the institutions, where their forms maintained links over time and across generations, where desires were domesticated by the rules, the current range of attitudes, opinions and signs tends to privilege openness (that horizontal and instantaneous sign identifying a generation to itself), to organize infidelity and return desire. Where precept, history, admiration and memory once committed people to reproduce, discouraged time wasting, instilled respect and defined the limits of the individual, today the internet, use of the remote to zap between identities, seem to offer everyone everything, right now, as and when they want it, and persuade every individual to be his or her own artwork. Where the structures used to pre-exist and outlive individuals, they are now expected to assemble their own ephemeral identities from the shifting mass of available, disposable structures and forms.

The advent of the body means that the possibility of a meaning disappears, along with any notion of a good, or an evil, ordered by an external truth. Good and evil are what is good or bad for the body, for its satisfaction, its desire, its long lifespan, its emotion, its sensations. Meaning gets swamped by rhythms, sounds, colours, the digital screen reality … belief in Manchester United, Johann Sebastian Bach or hip-hop has to do instead. It could be that madness is the only freedom left, in a society so reasonable, so comforting and protective. Or even that the fierce joy of drawing blood, the good fortune of killing an enemy, even just the commonplace richness of having an enemy to face, could be needed to remind us that we still exist.

The politics of life

> When the Japanese government instituted courses in good nutrition (*Asahi Shimbun*, March 2005), the left-wing parties posed a legitimate question: to what extent can the state involve itself in individual behaviour? The answer is obvious enough: since the principle of social support makes it the payer, and the payer calls the tune, the state is within its rights in refusing to enter a blind mutual arrangement, or as it were to buy a pig in a poke. But the question does not go far enough. If the new plan is to live well, is it not as important for the state to provide proper education in nutrition and health as in, for example, the three Rs? And how far should it go, the collective apprenticeship for that ill-defined objective that so obsesses us, the 'good life'?

Running a society no longer means suggesting a plan for tomorrow or the day after, it means guaranteeing everyone their physical capital and the best conditions for spending it, intensely and over a long period. It means ensuring the highest level of physical and moral well-being for a population, guaranteeing everyone their inheritance of long life. It means investing all the means of public authority in the abolition of such evils as cancer, disability, dangerous driving, genetic malformations, dietary risks, in warding off those that might be caused by phone-in services, mobile phones, video games and food substitutes: in banishing all fears. And it means defining life in terms of the qualities every man and woman has or will have the legal right to demand of their lives … or paying the compensation the courts will award them in case of default.

On the renewed territory of uncertainties, anxieties and fears, public action acquires a new, unprecedented, almost limitless legitimacy; when the field of our terrors extends from sex to calf's sweetbreads, CO_2 to airborne pollens in springtime, and foie gras to tropical deforestation, the territory is limitless, and limitless too is the power of those who will confront it. And the politician is required in this field, which may soon take on the supremacy that the economy—in the sense of currency, incomes, employment and social security—has held for 50 years. Governments will be judged on their success in extending life expectancy and preventing serious illnesses or infections linked to lifestyle. And they will do badly if they fail to understand the effects of innovation, progress and growth on lifestyles, health and individual and collective well-being. Politics will be the politics of the body. What we are seeing is not really a restriction of the public sphere and a decline in the politician's authority, but their departure to another terrain. So that, through being invisible, the intensity of the demands they expect may well mean a considerable extension of their activity, an extension prefigured by the tendency for public provision to create a market which is then hived off to private companies. Existing examples include the security market and the markets for dependent and home healthcare.

Should we imagine that 'health, safety, pleasure' has acquired the sort of meaning that 'liberty, equality, fraternity' has lost? Collective expectations, shaped by individual preferences, are going to change. Scientists, biologists, doctors, will be required to give concrete reality to the promises of a new historical condition, promises so far not kept by politics or economics: the promises of long life. And politicians to provide back-up, to define policies for bodies, for well-being, for security to ensure the peaceful enjoyment by all of that very long life. And local councillors to adapt the dream of a return to nature to the realities of urban planning … nature, yes, but with pavements, cable and high turnover. And jurists and politicians to help breach the frontiers—in place since secularism, universal suffrage and the civil code—between public and private, the domain of the self and the domain of others. And service providers and the new social intermediaries to devise new ways of being together, maturing and growing old, replacing the dilapidated forms of the family, the couple and the nation. And private companies and regulators to help substitute competing services, mutualized or not, for the exchange of unpaid services that used to take place in the family, couple or chosen entourage. And all of them, finally, to create conditions of confidence to prevent the overabundance of means from bringing an inability to act, long life from leading to an absence of projects, the invention of a new body from causing desire to decay and boredom and self-disgust to set in.

The advent of the body as a public object opens a new arena for competition between the regions of the world, which could well turn out decisive in the assertion of power by the US, the European Union, Russia, India, China and a few others. Management of demography and improving the quality of a population's health, consolidating its genetic capital, are economic and political weapons; weapons that will be used. The whole expanding array of genetic and biological resources will be used. They are and will remain one of the elements determining public choices and the conditions for acquiring and strengthening or maintaining power in the immediate future. The city-state of Singapore has taken the lead here by giving a grant to all graduate couples who choose to have a child, while taxing non-graduates wanting to do the same thing; the opposite of countries like France whose family policy, or what remains of it, is indiscriminate in its allocations and indifferent to the quality of the population. Eliminating the most widespread, disabling and costly pathologies; extending the duration of potentially active, economically productive life; overseeing a proper balance between the generations, based on their explicit collective preferences; piloting the evolution of population make-up using indicators of the level of integration, based on origin, monitored over several generations ... whatever the angle of approach, there cannot be much doubt that great emerging powers, India or China, both experiencing determining demographic movements of various kinds, will mobilize all their scientific resources and capacity for collective transformation to maximize their advantages—decisive ones perhaps—on this new front. It is enlightening to note the scale of effort being devoted to the mastery of living tissue by the US, concentrated on a few key areas of the appropriation and production of life, and its determination to increase its lead over other regions of the world in a domain that occupies 60 per cent of US research scientists and where the US alone accounts for 50 per cent of world investment and holds 65 per cent of all world patents. Suppose the twenty-first century turned out to be the century of the conquest of living matter, population management, and the body's policies...

The new body politic

Society is being made by the body alone, where it used to make the bodies that it appropriated, subjected, constrained. But what sort of society is being made by the bodies it makes no longer?

The sanitized society is already up and running, under the aegis of public health, reduction of vital risks, improvement of living conditions and prevention of collective pathologies. Because the body is becoming the favoured object of the law and the focus of mushrooming litigation, it is a favoured object of norms and rules, and of supervision. When politics becomes biological, the standardization of bodies is on the way. Developments in the law are combining with technical advances and changes in moral consciousness not just to allow, but to enjoin politicians to guarantee a right to be born without serious disabilities, formalized by the jurist

Marcela Iacub in the judgement by the Supreme Court of Appeal dated 17 November 2000, known as the Perruche judgement. The politician is faced with a new territory where his former terrible power of death—taking men to war, allowing capital punishment—is transformed into a power of life: defining the conditions under which an embryo can be permitted to reach birth, deciding whether it has the necessary biological qualities to live a good life.

Francis Crick, awarded the Nobel Prize for Medicine as co-discoverer of DNA, said in 1962 that no newborn child should be seen as human before undergoing a series of tests to assess its genetic endowment. This unexpected development in our civilization is a consequence of the intrusion of the law into diagnostics, and marks the entry of the quality of life into the right to life. All the means are already there. Thousands of genetic tests are available to identify possible hereditary anomalies or defects; the 'genetic quotient' provides a meaningful measure of the quality of human genomes, and can be used to predict individuals' liability to pathologies, their long-term health prospects and performances. In view of these capacities, intellectual arguments about the 'disposable man' (Gregory Benichou) or biological inequality will soon become redundant, for they ignore the fact that it has always been social recognition by the parents, more specifically by the father (ever since Abraham's sacrifice, in which filiation is founded on the name given by the father to the child, not on maternity or sexual relations), that gave the child the right to live. They ignore the fact that, in the absence of rules, but not of risk, today's medicine, when in doubt, falls back systematically on prescribing abortion. They forget the very high stakes of a society without disabilities, without premature deaths fated by heredity … and what doctor is not primarily concerned to reduce suffering, illness and death? Most of all, they forget that a humanity delivered from genetic misfortunes only amplifies and crowns its deliverance from pain, unplanned procreation, the propagation of epidemics; and marks a new stage in the conquest of the body as unique, and of life as its property.

The issue is no longer technical, but distinctly political; it consists of defining the qualities of genotype that confer the right to live. An obvious consequence of the devolution of rights to every member of society, along with the judicialization of medicine, this politics of life and the right to life represent a considerable and unexpected extension of the politician's prerogatives. Because in order to guarantee them, he also has to define and measure those elements of quality of life that will best enable every individual to get the most out of his or her allotted life-capital; in doing so, the politician is legitimized by the scale of public expenditure on an increasingly direct, specific and manifold intrusion into what used to be private life, on the irrefutable principle that 'he who pays the piper calls the tune'. The more socialized and mutualized a health system's spending becomes, the more inclined it will be to govern private behaviour. The politician's seizure, in the name of the common sanitary good, of private acts—lighting a cigarette, having one more for the road, ordering chocolate profiteroles, picking up a pretty or handsome stranger—transgresses categories once thought permanent, and for reasons no one finds strange. What we are seeing is a new public morality, in which well-being is the criterion of a good society, and virtuous living the criterion of good politics.

Morality of life choices

Jacques Chirac, as president of the French Republic, on many occasions intuitively claimed the political territory to come, by using in his speeches words new to political discourse: cancer, disability, health risk, road safety, screening, dependence, Alzheimer's, Parkinsonism, etc. And political action charged into the breach opened by the new behavioural morality to focus the public gaze on choices that had been private: drinking, smoking, eating too much, driving fast, etc. A new field of legitimacy from which it had once been excluded was opened for public action: the privacy of consumer behaviour. Because smokers, reckless drivers and inveterate boozers make society liable to costs whose mutualization—the propensity of public money to pay endlessly for the avoidable consequences of risky conduct—can be explained only by the bankruptcy of monitoring, prevention and follow-up systems.

This situation cannot last. Upward pressure on health expenditure, and the voters' intolerance of any increase in compulsory taxation, converge with fear of the 'eviction effect' that the absolute preference for health can have on other areas of economic activity; the regulation of expenditure through standardization or, if not, the sanctioning of individual behaviour, is already written into the public agenda of Western countries, albeit still veiled in the soft word 'prevention'. How could it not be, when by 2010 obesity is expected to become an unprecedented catastrophe in the US, leading to extra annual health costs estimated at more than $50 billion? And what country can continue to indulge the collective suicide implicit in tolerance for tobacco, soft drugs, alcohol and physical inactivity, what country can continue through social insurance to give every individual a blank cheque payable by society, and cashed by their doctor?

The body's spending frenzy crashes there, on the rocks of that new, responsible parsimony with money and with the self. The body is becoming dead to certain types of excess, experience or folly. AIDS, the wrecked metal coffins of Nimier or Camus on the autoroute, have seen to that. And Françoise Sagan with her Aston Martin dreams of artificial paradises, of casinos at dawn and the crazed expenditure of her body, departed just in time to avoid becoming something only later identified by today's public censors: a life delinquent.

The primacy of the body

> Late in 2004, biotechnological researchers achieved a major advance with the birth of the first hypoallergenic cat. Having noted that some candidates for the purchase of a cat were being put off by allergic reactions to their fur, the researchers solved the problem with a few genetic manipulations, resulting in a cat that would not cause allergies. All that remained was the production bottleneck; for the special cat, costing ten times the price of an ordinary cat, produced a flood of orders that would take several years to satisfy (the test-tube cat, maturing in a fortnight, being still in the future). Nevertheless, from the barkless dog to the non-caterwauling cat, astonishing prospects are open to the life manufacturers.
>
> On the North American market, in specialized pet shops in New York and other cities, all the animals sold are sterilized. Trying to make them reproduce is banned. It is sterility that lies behind the price of life. And to give life its price, death has to be produced.

This is not just another page in the great book of evolution, it is the end of an age. The slow evolution of the human species from anthropoid primates to hominids, then from homo erectus to homo sapiens, stretches over nearly two million years. The last 200,000 years have seen considerable transformation of the environment under the impact of human activity, but the art and manner of being born, maturing, reproducing, acting and dying stayed essentially the same. Mankind was powerless to change mankind. For countless thousands of years, since the first moves to preserve, to foresee and exchange, the economy struggled with scarcity.

Men dreamed of abundance, full granaries and security, without ever having the means for them except fleetingly, by accident, at random. And even the most recent major changes to the human body—increasing height, improvement of skeleton and musculature, most spectacular in regions of the world suffering from chronic nutritional deficiency—were only side-effects of human action to overcome scarcity or find protection against a hostile environment.

The free private enterprise economy has succeeded—more than succeeded—in doing what the socialisms had promised to do and had pursued, in China as in the Soviet Union, with all the means of virtually unlimited state power: it has developed a new man. It transformed not only the external forms of government and the superstructures of representation, but the physical and psychic condition of humanity. A new man emerged from that, and from him a new economy is appearing. And it is a *political* economy: the body's primacy will restore to collective choice the mastery over the economy it had lost during the early stages of global mercantilization. Ensuring respect for life, manoeuvring economic activity into taking all its external aspects, positive or negative, into account, and making their beneficiaries pay for them: the advent of the body calls for a new terrain, where the politician can impose its preferences and choices on the economy. In this respect, the advent of the body really does mean the end for all-powerful financial markets as we know them, just as it calls for a restoration of the political order to serve its well-being, its long life, its salvation.

None of the nineteenth-century thinkers who introduced the economic concepts we still use today would have doubted for a moment that our material ease, to them inconceivable, could only mean the end of the market economy and its evolution into something else for which there was (and incidentally still is) no name. Not for lack of vocabulary, but because of the paradoxical way economic rationality has prevailed among us with all the more force now that abundance reigns and the struggle against scarcity is becoming redundant. The economy, the market, is what has driven the Western project, born under the sign of reason, the master-key to universalism and individuation. For the economy was all that upheld reason in our relation to reality and to others, and is all that remains of rule and law in a nature that has otherwise disappeared. The masters of suspicion undermined our physical, psychic and moral certainties; the market economy reinstated the truth principle that we need in order to communicate, to compare, to exchange ... to live, in a word. Amid overabundance, peace, riches, it has been all that upheld reason in the world of ideologies, that opposed it without rocking its foundations, and all that remained of logic between separate individuals; it has been the only thing that unites, the only common language between those who no longer share anything else, the only reason to act for those who have no other... The myths and rituals have disappeared everywhere else: only the economy has been able to impose their magic on us, and unite us in sacrificing to its vanished reason. All that is finished. An economics of well-being, governed by the primacy of the body, is embarking on a vast reordering of values, prices, preferences and standards. This shift, emerging from the advent of the body, places health, well-being and physical integrity above the economy. A time of collective preferences and choices has come once again. It is going to organize the life market under the aegis of the advent of the body.

The price of life

> Most of our contemporaries will never own anything more costly than their own bodies, given the indemnities paid by insurance companies in connection with recent air disasters (more than a million dollars per victim). *Pretium doloris*, the price of the body, is increasing constantly under pressure of two simultaneous developments in the law. The first is a tendency to classify as serious or total disabilities physical flaws that would once have been considered minor, especially when they are damaging to people's integrity or self-image, to their beauty; where a disability level of 25 to 40 per cent would have been registered 20 years ago, invalidity rated at 80 or 100 per cent would often be awarded today. The second development is the increasing indemnities awarded after incidents causing death; following the terrorist attack of 11 September 2001, the minimum price of a body is nudging $800,000, and can be a great deal more. The price of life has risen much more steeply over the last five years than that of other assets like shares, property or art!

In losing life one loses everything. That old saying acquires a fierce new relevance when long life, the 'last generation' syndrome and the end of history dissipate the obligation to accumulate and the hope of living on through one's heritage; it announces the primacy of life over the economy. Above money, above capital and property, there is the body. The body that does the living, and that is unique, is finally all that remains rare, restricted ... for it continues to die. By that token it is the only thing that resists, the only thing that escapes the market, the only thing that is recalcitrant to an exchange or price. For life can be bought, but no one sells it.

That reality has found recent expression in the abolition of capital punishment from the range of sentences pronounced by the courts in 'civilized' countries (with the significant exception of the US). French rhetoric was especially enlightening on the meaning of this abolition, a significant transformation in the relations between government, the law and bodies. Behind the necessary public debate on a penalty almost never used, probably ineffective and undoubtedly pointless, along with the all-important assessment of the possibility of judicial error that makes it monstrous, the arguments laid before the French parliament in 1981 (notably in the Senate debate which ended with a vote in favour of the abolition proposed by the Justice minister, Maître Robert Badinter) took a singular turn 20 years later, especially when amplified by an infectiously hysterical view of those countries still practising capital punishment. It amounts to an assertion that nothing is worth more than a human life; that civilization, culture, values, should yield first place to respect for life. What used to be sacred was the soul, for eternity was at stake. Bodies were tortured and burned alive so that their souls might be saved for eternity. We have lost eternity; the body is sacred now; there is nothing at stake important enough to justify doing any harm to it. Indeed it is hard to avoid the conclusion that the lives of our enemies are more precious than whatever they might want from us.

Twenty years on, in the light of the precautionary principle, mounting environmental worries, and direct evidence that human health is compromised by industrial operations, that assertion seems prophetic. To say that life is worth more than anything else does not really mean abandoning the long-established state privilege of the monopoly of armed force (although it will help speed the process of privatization of force; France already has more security professionals in the private sector than in the police and gendarmerie combined). It breaks with a thread of another kind that runs through the whole history of the West: the view that civilization really is worth more than the lives of its enemies, that civilization amounts to something greater than individual life; that progress justifies the sacrifice of human life.

Exhaustion of the world

> When the British imported tea cultivation to Sri Lanka (then Ceylon) and were terracing the hillsides around Nuwara Eliya to establish their extensive tea estates there, they disturbed the leopards whose hunting territory covered the region. The leopards started to attack and kill the young women tea-pickers who went to work on the terraces every morning, among thick bushes that reached shoulder height. The Buddhist Sinhalese, respectful of life, solved the problem by sending men through the terraces ringing hand-bells at daybreak, to drive the leopards out for the day. A few attacks still occurred, arousing a resigned compassion for the victims; leopards have the right to live too, after all. It is interesting to speculate on what might have happened if the Americans had conquered Sri Lanka; probably, in the name of efficiency and security, every single leopard in Sri Lanka would have been eliminated. But without leopards, would there still be a Sri Lanka?

The primacy of bodies and the absolute obligation to protect human life are combining with the disappearance of nature's gifts to transform the profitability of economic activity, in particular industrial operations, and ultimately to disrupt the structure of prices and revenues: overabundant human labour and intelligence will be worth less, while scarce, tightly controlled products will be worth more ... and nothing—land, fish, game, fruit, water, nothing at all—will be available from nature free for the taking.

This shift is no less than a matter of survival. It is mistaken to think that the growth of activity in the developed countries has had the unfortunate secondary effect of exhausting natural resources. The guzzling of natural resources made growth possible, since the industries that exhausted the soil, polluted the atmosphere and used up air, water and space at will generally recovered their investments not through their methods or commercial acumen, or through the skill and labour of their workers, but by appropriating, using and abusing nature. Suppliers of cement and building materials, chemicals industries, farmers and agro-food industrialists, are among the beneficiaries of the world's benevolent generosity, as well as our collective indolence in failing to gauge the damage they were doing. With half the cranes in the world busy transforming the skylines of Chinese cities, the consumption of one major gift—space—is accelerating visibly; and when the sky above Beijing is hidden for six months at a time by smoke and pollution the price of air, an essential that no one has ever had to pay for, is rising.

The destruction of the world as a gift, as abundant nature, has reached its climax with the appropriation of living tissue. For it is deluded to imagine that the remarkable prospects held out by the biotechnology companies that have accumulated patents and are starting to rake in their first royalties are primarily the product of human inventive genius; for the most part they correspond to the private appropriation of cells and biological processes which used to be generally available but are now being brought into the world of the market by the law. The legal actions being brought by indigenous communities for recovery of title to genes or species captured on their territory (for example, the government of Kenya is suing over a bacterium filched from the region of Lake Turkana and patented by an American company as a bleach for jeans) should be taken seriously, for they concern the ownership of the world and the creation of meta-ownerships of living matter dispossessing the territories where that life had grown and reproduced. Likewise, it is mistaken to imagine that the growth rates attained by India, China, or Indonesia—8 to 10 per cent annually, with peaks of 15 to 18 per cent in some areas—really represent rates of expansion of activity; they indicate firstly that subsistence-level activity, artisanal or not, is being brought into the market framework and monetarized; that labour, especially women's labour, is being misappropriated by the salaried classes; and that new enterprises effectively enjoy extensive subsidies in the use, and often the pillage, of the available resources—timber, water, space (especially where dams are involved), air (atmospheric pollution in South-East Asia is such that the monsoon cycle is being disrupted)—which ensure high returns on invested capital, at least in the short term. It is equally wrong to think that the spirit of initiative, the organization of the market economy, the commitment and sometimes the genius of entrepreneurs, are the sole or main reasons for the fabulous growth of some businesses; the free and uncosted inputs of every sort, social and environmental, which have benefited private as well as public enterprises, the unlimited use of natural and structural capital by Western companies yesterday and Asian ones today, are at least as responsible for value creation in the past century. It would be closer to the truth to see the return on finance capital as coming primarily from the liquidation of natural capital first in the industrialized countries, then in the planet at large. The continuing use of natural capital may be problematic, and the use of structural capital may be limited by the breakdown in the transmission and renewal of such capital. But the substitution of the market for nature in the production of the self, the body, desire and satisfaction should provide new opportunities for enterprise, appropriation and enrichment.

A new price paradigm

> The health risk posed by asbestos has been recognized since the beginning of the last century. The incidence of asbestosis was tolerated in the name of efficiency, added to the list of professional hazards, and indemnified under the terms of a political, economic and trade union agreement that prevailed until 1995, essentially identical to the ones covering miner's lung (silicosis) and similar conditions. By the end of the 1990s, however, following the scares over blood contaminated with HIV or hepatitis, mad cow disease and avian influenza, the agreement foundered under pressure from a public opinion that now saw the body as a sanctuary of the sacred, and no longer accepted that money or economic activity could justify the threat of illness, physical disability or death. The right to live in a stable environment posing no avoidable health risks figures in the environmental Charter. The precautionary principle goes further, holding the state accountable for the health consequences of every decision it has made ... or not made. The effect is already apparent: the number of innovative products made available to the medical profession halved between 1992 and 2002 (Claudie Haigneré, minister of Research, 2003), while research budgets, public and private, doubled worldwide over the same period. So that people are expecting more and getting less, here in the West anyway, while Chinese, Indian and Israeli laboratories race ahead unhampered by such concerns.

The Renaissance, and even more the age of the Enlightenment, were marked by the obsession with naming; nomenclature, classification, the dictionary, were means of progress; they aided communication and exchange, and more importantly led to the definition of categories, classes and groups, and explored the structures that linked or separated them.

Like the twentieth century, but even more so, the twenty-first is being born under the sign of price; what has been named, classified, listed, numbered and counted has to have a price these days. This passion for putting a price on everything, on every relation, every asset, every body even, is no mere passing enthusiasm; it is the condition for entry to the universal, and the means of participation in development.

The sterilization of nature, the appropriation of living matter and the exhaustion of the soil are putting an end to the era of free resources for enterprise; the advent of the body means that its days are numbered, and heralds the end for all the free external inputs that fed growth and generated its financial expression, increasing wealth. Industry will no longer escape its share of the collective costs it imposes on the territories and communities where it produces, transforms, sells and employs. Bhopal, Seveso, the Amoco Cadiz and Chernobyl sounded the death-knell for free gifts of that kind; no matter if the party goes on for another five or ten years: the die is already cast. A world grown small will not tolerate for much longer enterprises that behave abroad in ways they do not behave at home. The politics of bodies, of long life and caution, demands the standardization of decision-makers, of their behaviour and the principles behind their decisions; competing private enterprises will not escape it. The end of an economy based on liquidating free gifts from the world's abundance, its death-throes already signalled by recent excesses in the financial and stock markets, is approaching. It signifies that the impact of all the reorganizations, restructurings and relocations put in train since the 1990s will have to be weighted by the internalization of all cost-free external inputs, sufficient in itself to reduce in many cases, and sometimes wipe out, the profits of industrial companies. What will the cost price of sand be if every quarry has to pay the full price of damage to the landscape? How will French agriculture and agro-industry manage if water to irrigate maize in the South-West has to be bought at the true cost of its replacement or purification?

These observations do not arise from any concern for the environment; they follow from the primacy of the body. People who hope to live a good life for 100 years, in rich countries, or who hope to attain happiness defined by physical well-being, in other countries, are not going to tolerate a small world rendered threatening by economic side-effects and the hazards of growth; still less will they tolerate being marked in their bodies, dragged back into the world of suffering, short lifespan and physical deprivation by the effects of industry. The time is not far off when businesses, instead of fearing legal definition of the limits of what is due, will welcome it; for they will be confronted with violent demands and a prioritization of health leading to an explosion of the *pretium doloris* ... the process is already well advanced.

This shift announces the birth of a new paradigm of price formation, in which the impact of economic and other activity on human life, health and well-being will be a factor in determining its value. The need for such a development is becoming apparent in a confused, contradictory way, masked by a flurry of new terms—'sustainable development', 'social responsibilities of enterprise', 'business ethics', 'professional code of practice'—widely, and very misguidedly, invoked as ways to circumvent the law, excuses for doing nothing. For the societies they cheat and reassure at such small cost are putting themselves in danger. The demand is not moral, or intellectually soothing, or the expression of a new ideology; it is a demand for survival. Amid the disorder and confusion caused by the extension of political power and authority into so many new areas of life, a new public order is being established, and established as judge, guide and guarantor of all activity in the name of the body and the virtuous life. The past two decades have seen impassioned debates over the ozone layer and the increase in skin cancers (as many as half of Australia's young adult surfers may be affected), global warming, the extinction of the planet's remaining wild mammals, the pathologies caused by asbestos, tobacco and chemical dust and fumes, food chain disasters (from BSE to avian influenza), the statistical increase in illnesses arising from atmospheric pollution … if Western public opinion has learned anything from these issues, it is that life itself is at stake.

Far more than any anxiety over the coming shortage of resources and the future cost of products today still free or widely affordable, fears for the quality of life for today's adults and tomorrow's children leave little room for doubt on the arbitrations that will be made. Businesses will have to bear an increasing proportion of what used to be called social security, and will be renamed as the social responsibility of economic decision-makers for the external effects of their operations. They will also find themselves squeezed between multiplying claims, in this health domain, from their employees, the customers using their products or services, and the populations among which their activities take place. Widespread closures, relocations and reclassifications are to be expected when the price of life is included in the accounts; when enterprises have to account internally for all the free external resources they have enjoyed for centuries, that they consumed and misused in the last century in the grandiose and ridiculous process of destroying the world as a free gift and source of abundance.

A new capitalism

> We have finished with the overabundance of human life, with women giving birth to 12 or 15 babies so that three or four might survive the terrible selection ordeal of childhood: sickness, abandonment, miserly, careless or incompetent nursing, domestic accidents, assorted brutalities, exacted a frightful toll among children under ten. The life principle was adored, bodies casually abandoned. Now we adore the body but no longer respect the life principle. The most meticulous attentions, the most delicate treatments, nothing seems too much in caring for a body that is born, that has matured, that can receive and give pleasure; the worship of life has disappeared and been replaced by worship of sterility, the condition of its scarcity and its price. It will fall to this century to manage and cost something that no previous century has had to cost or manage: life.

The coming capitalism is going to concentrate unprecedented means on the human body. The most obvious area of change is the opening up of investment in health, procreation and the production of bodies as a leading economic sector for the near future. As it leaves the domain of nature, human life enters that of the law, business and the market. New rights and new forms of property are in play: investing in what has never before been an investment, devising forms of private ownership for what has never before been anyone's property, assessing cash flows to cost what has never before been subject to price, exchange or demand. With the wishes and preferences of potential clients still at the stage of hesitant murmurs, the life-production market, the market in repair and renewal of the body, the membership and identity market have already taken on enough substance to attract the attention of the world's biggest companies as well as the effort of innovators and risk-takers.

When the health division of General Electric includes a world-leading supplier of medical analyses, when a pharmaceutical group takes control of a string of biotechnology firms, when the cosmetics giant L'Oréal homes in on the pre- and post-operative care markets, when providers of management facilities are working on the offer of home-care services for dependent or bedridden individuals, what occurs is not so much innovation or product development as the transfer of investment from mature activities, with limited prospects, to activities with high or very high added value and good development potential. After the classification of hospitals and clinics by performance and sanitary quality had become widespread, the travel assistance organization Mondial Assistance published in 2004 the first guide comparing 800 health establishments in 108 countries, marking a new stage by putting health systems in direct competition. In another innovation, the French subsidiary of the German insurer Allianz supplies its doctors with a directory enabling them to choose between treatment on the spot and repatriation, in the event of a health incident to the insured. But a new development of the promising medical tourism market is also approaching, no longer from poor countries to the hospitals of rich ones, but driven by citizens from the North, faced with the impoverishment or mediocrity of their own systems, going elsewhere to find as cash customers what their social insurance does not cover.

New combinations of activity are on the cards, anticipating the removal of the barriers separating the demands of health and well-being, nutrition and beauty, security and membership, entertainment and moral comfort; new forms of activity too, whether business-oriented or not. And, pervading everything else, the intrusion of the market, of competition and prices, into areas that used to be outside the economy or considered public property, has begun. For the invention of the body also signifies, in many respects, its privatization.

In one way or another, all the consequences of economic activities on health, well-being and quality of life are going to catch up with those responsible. The 'green' revolution in California had the immediate effect of making any future politics, any future economics, a politics or economics of survival. Business is going have to pay for what it has never before been required to pay for (and what not one economic decision-maker has paid for so far), most particularly in the social domain, which the precautionary principle promises to reinterpret from top to bottom. In France, as elsewhere in Europe, labour law was constructed in the struggle against the exploitation of workers. During the final decade of the twentieth century, psychologization of labour issues caused a tilt towards preventing victimization: ensuring that the worker—that victim by nature—is spared anything that might aggravate the situation. But the tools for monitoring work content and output are inadequate if required to define, in order to penalise them, 'moral harassment', 'unjustified pressure', 'moral undermining' or simply 'stress'. Danone will no more escape than McDonald's from the absolute requirement that its products, and profit margins, remain at least compatible with long-term well-being. Alcohol producers, then producers of food, beauty products, body accessories, will be subjected one by one to constraints, warnings, proceedings analogous to those that curb the tobacco companies; worse still, they will be made to limit their promises to what their products can achieve. All threats or damage to the body's well-being and fulfilment will be exposed, evaluated and penalized; all activities directly or indirectly affecting health and fitness will be subjected to enforced and supervised standards, at the end of a change—favourable to planetary democracy—that fine-tunes the new governance to the service of collective preferences, disrupting in the process the conditions for economic calculation and production of added value. Business is going to subsidize the state of its surroundings on an increasing scale. It is not saying much to observe that there will be winners and losers from the ending of free inputs; environmental costs have already led to some relocations and deindustrialization in Western countries. Soon, their societal costs will generate a new wave of geographical transfers, innovation in products and marketing procedures, range revision and facelifted offerings, as some go struggling to the wall under constraints that are fatal to them, while others seize unforeseen opportunities by anticipating the new collective preferences, and capitalizing on those new public assets that the body's primacy demands.

At the end of a strange detour, collective preferences for health, life and well-being are on the point of restoring the political, involving a measure of choice and will, to its former place above the economic. The demand for health and well-being, the dream of history stopping and bodies being eternal, are consistent enough for a new political product to be constructed from them, able to impose standardized rules on competing firms across all markets; consistent enough for the resulting new legitimacy to establish a political administration with some control over the economy.

Following the advent of the body, the economy, the market and financial markets will no longer be our truth system, if they ever were. Their system may have been prepared to suck the world dry, but does not exhaust reality. It will gain a new power from its new legitimacy; bringing the calculation of added value into the production of well-being. It is by contributing in its own way to the advent of the glorious, sovereign, protected body, by working out the price attached to the body's primacy, that the market system can become the instrument of the new politics, the one that counts: the politics of bodies.

From One Body to Another, No Change

That is where we are. At the end of a secular evolution, the body is now real only to be transfigured: to escape from reality through processes of fabrication. Every individual's own body is his primary object of desire, most valuable possession and sole inheritance, the accumulation of experiences his only true expense. While medical, psychiatric and aesthetic artifice act as insurance against a setback that might restore to the body its share of reality, of hazard or risk. Even psychoanalysis itself, in its dive into the abysses, comes up against that dense wish, in whose formation it has played no small part: the wish to produce oneself, understood as the wish to be detached from one's environment, heritage and origins.

After the intoxicating excitement of the ownership of the body and the production of bodies, we remain suspended between two eternities, of the species and of the soul. And we are discovering, to our confusion, that the much-vaunted advances meant to liberate mankind from its connections also release deeper and more harmful impulses. Undertaking to establish the body, its well-being and its satisfaction, as our system of truth, tells us nothing about the society being formed by the advent of the body. Looking down from above on God's plan for the world, on the grandeur of nations, on progress towards a better world, we are seized by vertigo at the thought of this reign that chooses us more than we choose it, with its mechanisms, its Court, its compulsory rituals; and this truth system imposing itself on the economy and the market, just as it imposed itself on the gods and the politician, says nothing of the bodies it is inventing, which will never be the same again as a result of having no law but themselves. The mechanism of life is out of control, and its instructions have been lost. The separation, the freedom, the expenditure of bodies are accompanied by a collectivization of imagination, of the irrational, of representations and opinions exemplified in France by the rise of dissidence and censorship. Bodies are free because representations, opinions and commitments are enclosed in processes that standardize and order them, the internet being the most striking example.

We are there. In the contract society no one can sing the *Internationale* or *Le temps des cérises*. Dreaming about revolution is as forbidden as making it, now that the order of contracts is closing in. It may not be the end of history writ large, but it is surely the end of the history the peoples of the West were making or trying to make, and that some still recite on election eve, at meetings, to forget ageing, to deny it.

The exit from modernity is close. The era so called, marked by a sometimes frenetic effort to sever ties and pursue mobility, liquidity and detachment, will soon be superseded. There will be no return, that impossible return yearned for by nostalgics for a situation that never really existed. There will be reinvention: of a relation to reality that the market will not exhaust; of interpersonal relations that satisfaction will not exhaust; of a registration in time that will acquire a unique value by enduring.

This situation upsets the order of probabilities affecting life, provision for the future, for disability. Risk used to be risk of death. The only true risk now is becoming the risk of a reduced life, calculated in terms of the damage represented by the loss of space: the scale of the reduction. Anything that attacks, dilapidates or destroys is intolerable; and any damage done from outside ought to be restored, using money as a means to provide living space. Risk used to be risk of impoverishment. The real risk now is of becoming incapable of feeling, unfit for any human relationship, so wide has the disjunction grown between reason and emotion, logic and affect.

Religion maintained a vertical connection between God and humans, like the one between humans and the sky; and it regulated the horizontal links between humans. The market came to substitute its universal and accountable reason as rule, language and mode of exchange. It also linked what had never been linked before, connected those who had never thought that they had anything in common. That link is broken. The market still deals with the horizontal link but now it is the body that connects with other things, that establishes frontiers and reinvents separateness; because it is complete, and so long as it is complete, it becomes the face of God, of otherness, of the same and the other. Extreme fatigue, the idea of serious illness, of extreme old age that bends the spine or makes the heart flutter, are my sole remaining links with something recalcitrant to the credit card, resistant to any contract. I accomplish myself, I consume myself, I claim myself, I am.

Alone, the body remembers that it is finite; alone, it roots us in its limits, our last frontier (for how long?); and even if—especially if—it forgets, the body alone still prevents us from being God to ourselves and others.

Index